S0-CBX-586

In the valley of the shadow of death

DADS DON'T DIE

BY ROD BUZZARD

Unless otherwise indicted, all scripture quotations are taken from the King James Version of the Bible.

DAD'S DON'T DIE!

Copyright ⓒ 1993 Light for Life Ministries, Inc.

ISBN 1-0-9638378-0-X

Published by Light for Life Ministries, Inc.
P. O. Box 755
Auburn, IN 46706

All rights reserved under International Copyright Law. This publication may not be reproduced, stored in a retrieval system, or transmitted in whole or in part, in any form or by any means, electronic, mechanical, photocopying, recording or otherwise, without prior express written permission of the Publisher.

Printed in the United States of America.

248.86
B989d

L. I. F. E. Bible College
LIBRARY
1100 COVINA BLVD
SAN DIMAS, CA 91773

DEDICATION

This book is dedicated
to those who are now
suffering in their
valley with cancer;

that this book will be
a source of encouragement
and blessing to you.

$5.00

9-00

1145840

L.I.F.E. Bible College
LIBRARY
1100 COVINA BLVD
SAN DIMAS, CA 91773

FOREWORD

BY: DR. PAUL E. PAINO

There is no testimony without a test. The following pages contain a powerful testimony! The experience that Pastor Rod Buzzard shares will be a comfort to any who are called upon to suffer or to go through some hard and trying experience in life!

I urge you to read each page carefully and prayerfully. You will feel the pain. You will be deeply moved and affected. There will be moments that you will identify with the writer. There are moments of humor, intrigue, transparency and often deep and meaningful feelings.

Over the years I have watched Rod. I knew him when he came to Christ. I watched him grow in the grace and knowledge of the Lord. He and Alison are faithful, committed, and dedicated servants of the Lord. They pastor a fine and successful congregation. With prayer and years of hard work, they have built a solid church fellowship in Auburn, Indiana.

Through Rod's "valley experience", I saw him fight with determination and faith. His character was developed. He became more sensitive to the hearts of people. He is a faithful man with a powerful testimony. He is a good pastor with a caring heart! I recommend this book to you. You will be blessed. This testimony will help you. God is the God of valleys!

"DADS DON'T DIE"

In the valley of the shadow of death

TABLE OF CONTENTS

"DADS DON'T DIE"

NOT NOW

I was enjoying the few minutes of relaxation my husband and I were spending together. It seemed that lately our lives had been so busy that we had no time for ourselves, for our two children, or time alone for each other. It was so nice to take some time out just for us.

Rod's head was on a pillow in my lap. It was a beautiful May afternoon, the sun was shining and I was reading to him from one of my women's magazines. He was being patient with me, as I read little clips to him. Then I came across an article that made him sit up and take notice. The article was referring to testicular cancer, found in young men between the ages of 14 and 40 years of age. It usually began with a lump in the testicle. If not treated by radiation or chemotherapy, it could be very deadly.

I knew that Rod had found such a lump, but he wasn't sick, and it didn't bother him so why see a doctor. The article had scared him, and right away his comment was; "Let's make an appointment as soon as possible to see the doctor." So I did. After being sent to two different doctors, the urologist said he really didn't see a big problem, but that the only way to know, would be to do a biopsy of the lump, which was smaller than a pea. Rod was then scheduled to go in as an outpatient. Both of us were very glad, because there was so much work to be done at the church and with the building of our new home.

My first prayer was "God, NOT NOW! You know how busy we are. We don't have time for this."

Hand in hand, we headed to the hospital in hopes that this would be the end of the whole ordeal. We knew it would probably be no more than an hour. But it seemed like forever. The doctor appeared through the door and stood directly in front of me. "Mrs. Buzzard." "Yes, that's me," I said. "Everything went real well, Rod is doing fine," the doctor reported. He said the lump really didn't look cancerous, but for precautionary methods they went ahead and removed the testicle, just to be safe.

I knew Rod would be "thrilled" to hear that news. He said they would have to wait for the final report from the pathologist and we should just give his office a call in a few days. They would be glad to let us know the results of the tests. What a relief! God is good!

Two days later, I received a phone call from the doctor's office asking if my husband and I could come in and meet with the doctor concerning the results of his tests. Fear gripped my heart. The doctors said I should call them. It was a day early. Why would we have to go in to the doctor's office if it wasn't something serious? Please God, NOT NOW. You know there's work to be done. You need my husband.

The next twenty-four hours were torment. I had such a hard time keeping my mind on things that needed to be accomplished. I tried my hardest to put my trust in God. After all, I had been a Christian for sixteen years. God had never failed me, not one time; and He wasn't going to fail me this time.

The next day we walked into the doctor's personal office, sat in the two chairs across from his desk. We tried to act as normal as possible, even though we both were very nervous. Then we heard the word everyone fears of hearing. CANCER!

"You have what is called testicular cancer, a very rare cancer found in young males. A very deadly cancer if not treated, but if treated, a very high cure rate." I hung my head and my mind began to go a mile a minute. I was very familiar with the ugly word, cancer. My sister had been diagnosed with a cancerous brain tumor. She had been fighting for her life. My younger sister had been diagnosed with malignant melanoma (skin cancer) and after going through surgery, had conquered the cancer. I myself had a precancerous condition and had a hysterectomy. The word cancer was not new to my vocabulary, but now my own husband.

It couldn't be. What about the kids, the church, our house? I can't do this alone. We are a team. I took a deep breath, seconds had passed, but it seemed like years. The doctor continued, "We would like to send you to the Indianapolis Medical Center to see what kind of treatment they would recommend. Would it work out for you to leave Monday?" Monday! This is Friday and you want us just to stop all of our plans, I thought to myself.

As we left the doctor's office, I tried to be strong but I felt my strength leaving. Not a word was said for fear of just totally losing it. As we walked outside, there seemed to be so much hustle and bustle all around us. Cars going here and there, people conversing with one another, kids laughing. How could this be? Don't you people know that my husband has cancer! I wanted to yell, "STOP everyone! Stop what you're doing. Look over here. My husband just found out he has cancer. Aren't you concerned?" The whole world seemed to be going on it's merry way while we stood still. GOD, are you there! God, not now! Please, not now!

MOVING ON

The next few weeks were busy ones as we frantically worked to put things in order. Telling our families was very difficult. How do you tell the people you love; your mom, dad, brother, and sister that you have cancer. I remember telling my parents was extremely hard, especially because of all of the cancer in our family. I know I sounded very strong and confident. They were very supportive, and willing to help in any way they could.

I knew that it was going to be stressful and emotional for Rod to tell his mother and father. But it had to be done. They knew he had had a biopsy and was waiting for the test results, and I am sure they were in no way prepared for the word "cancer". Who is? We certainly weren't. The call was made. I stayed in the other room, but I was listening as he began to explain the results.

I heard him begin to sob, uncontrollably! I knew his mother was probably doing the same on the other end. As he pulled himself together, I heard him say, "Mom, I'm going to be fine, everything will be fine." He hung the phone up. We held each other and we both cried. There was comfort in our embrace. We didn't want to let it go.

Telling our children seemed to be less emotional, than in telling our parents. Our son, Josh, was fourteen and our daughter, Sarah, was nine. Children just seem to take things as they come. They knew Dad would be okay. After all, DADS DON'T DIE!

The church family was so supportive and willing to fill in the gap in any way they could. When part of the body is hurting, the whole body hurts. I knew they hurt, but I also knew they were people of faith.

Rod was so concerned about the church. After all, he

had founded the work and had been pastoring for eleven years. He had never been away for any long periods of time.

That all happened on Friday. Monday, we drove down to the medical center. They began more testing to see what type of treatment would be best for him. Our friends, Dennis and Carol, went with us. It was so nice to know that we could lean on their friendship at such a time as this.

After much testing we were told that Rod would have to have three courses of chemotherapy, which consisted of one week on, two weeks off. He would have to be hospitalized during his treatments because they would be giving him his "chemo" intravenously in high doses. He would become very sick, lose all his hair and because of some of the drugs, have short-term memory loss. But, they would do their best to make him as comfortable as possible.

I began to realize that summer would be over by the time his treatments were finished. I couldn't take the time with the kids that we had planned. There were all kinds of little odds and ends to be finished at the house. How would it all get done?

I knew from the beginning that God had a plan. I realized I must lean on Him! My strength must come from the Lord!! I had no other source but Him. God, what is it you want to show me through this experience? Your ways and thoughts are higher than ours.

I wasn't sure what to expect. The nurses were so good at trying to help me understand how Rod would feel. They let me know that within the first hour of his treatment he would begin vomiting, which they would try to control with medication. He would not be much company and he probably would not have much of an appetite.

If you can imagine your worst day of the flu and multiply that 100 times, that would be what he would feel.

They let him rest for two weeks at home, and then back to the hospital! Then, he would begin the process all over again.

By the end of the first week, Rod's strength was gone. I had spent the week taking care of him--bathing him, washing his hair, shaving him, and dressing him. He was barely able to make it to the car. The two hour drive home was a quiet one. Rod hardly said two words.

The man who just a week ago on the same trip was full of conversation and life, had made a total turn around. He was lifeless. I began to realize for the first time that this summer was going to be a lonely one.

For over fourteen years, my husband had been a strong leader of our family, and now I began to realize things would be different. Could I really handle this? Could I really become the strong one? Even though I don't like being alone, deep down inside I knew I could by walking one day at a time with God.

After all ... DADS DON'T DIE!

Alison Buzzard

INTRODUCTION

"You will die within two years!"

What? Did he really say that? I could see my cold body lying stiff in the casket with a plastic smile as my widow and children stood in grieving unbelief. Some were saying, "He looks natural." Others were commenting that he was so young.

That was the beginning of my difficult battle with cancer. A battle that I have won, but not without the help of many wonderful people and the Lord!

All people do face difficulties. It is a fact of life. No one finds trouble enjoyable because such seasons produce pain.

However, in every journey of life there are certain valleys appointed by God. These valleys have purpose and a positive product for each traveler.

With the pain and challenges there are those whom God sends into your life to make a difference, those who support and care as you walk through the time of testing. Friends and family produce strength.

Alison, my wife is one of those people. She suffered in different ways than I. The uncertainty of my future health and the responsibilities of a home and family weighed on her. The taxing schedule of my treatment and care was demanding. But I watched the emotional upheaval rebuild special strength, commitment, and determination. I express deep gratitude to a courageous and faithful wife who stood with me through this serious crisis time in my life!

Joshua and Sarah are the bright spot of my life. Though they were young, they held up my hands spending many days in hospitals when they would have rather been on the ball field or riding their bikes. But again, they were unselfish and loving. My love and appreciation for them has deepened through this experience.

My mother and father set aside their interest to help and to support. Good parents offered regular encouragement. I felt their concern and love.

Calvary Chapel of Auburn, Indiana demonstrated grace and mercy throughout the ordeal. The loving people chose to not only stand with us, but constantly sent expressions of love and support. The fellowship of the people brought more comfort and strength than all the money and possessions that the world has to offer.

Calvary Ministries Inc. Int'l, the fellowship of churches that I serve under, holds a great place of love and esteem in my heart for the part they played. This group of ministers demonstrated that they truly cared. Special thanks to our Bishop, Dr. Paul E. Paino and to his wife. Their counsel and love gave the insight and strength to turn many critical corners. Thank You.

Most of all, I appreciate the Lord who has been my best Friend throughout my life. He was there to provide every need and to grant wisdom in every decision. Even when I could not see or feel His presence, He remained faithful. Thank you, Lord, for your faithfulness.

God never allows anything to come into our lives but what He has a plan on how it can be used for good. We should never confuse the facts of life with the acts of God. Cancer was a fact of life for me, but God's grace, love, and wisdom were the acts that brought me through!

There are many advantages that God grants us as we walk our pilgrimage of life through the valley from one mountain top to another. This is my story of my battle with cancer and the benefit that came to my life.

Chapter One

THE VALLEY OF SHOCK

"Without a cure, you will die within two years!" It rang in my ears.

Wow, I couldn't believe what I just heard. It isn't supposed to work this way. I was young and a Christian. I tried to be faithful to the church and ministry. I strived to be a loving father and a good husband.

As the doctor continued, he explained that a cure had been developed, but that it was a painful, complicated, and a time-consuming process. First, there was surgery to diagnose the stage of the cancer.

Since this was testicular cancer, it first spread to the lymph system in the lower abdomen, then to the lungs, and from there to the brain and other organs of the body. The only way that they could discover how far it had spread microscopically was to make an incision from the groin to the sternum. They would then remove a hundred or so lymph nodes and examine each one under the microscope to see if there were any cancerous cells.

This surgery would last for eight to ten hours. After it was over, it would take one week in the hospital to get on my feet, and six weeks of recovery at home.

The process, called "staging", would only be the beginning because it determined the amount of chemotherapy I would receive. As soon as my strength returned they would begin two to four courses of "chemo".

Each course of "chemo" was to be given aggressively. They would hospitalize me for five days and put me on intravenous fluids to prevent my kidneys from failing during treatments. Then, they would fill me with the highest dosage of "chemo" possible without killing me.

This course would result in horrible side effects of nausea, skin blotches, and a dangerous lowering of my white blood count. It would take 14 days to recover. Then, they would hospitalize me again and start another course.

Since hospitals made me feel uncomfortable and needles were the number one fear of my life, this was not good news. But, I was thankful for the hope they offered.

God is good and He was very good to me! As a young man I was experiencing the successes of life. All that an individual could want, seemed to be at my fingertips.

At the age of thirty-two, the country church that we founded at the age of twenty had grown to a congregation of four hundred people. The Lord helped us to build a nice facility, and a spirit of worship and evangelism was on the hearts of the saints.

Life was good and the ministry was flourishing. My whole existence lay before me beaming with potential. So it did not seem possible that I could be in this place hearing what was just said.

It all began when I noticed a lump just the size of a pea while showering one day. I reassured myself that I did not need to worry.

Several weeks later the lump was still there. Each time I pondered the situation, I wondered if it could be cancer. But, I fought away those thoughts. I just didn't want to believe it was possible.

I remember sitting in the doctors' lounge. It all seemed so sterile. I was alone and it was time to hear the doctor's opinion. As I looked at the brown carpet on the floor and the beige walls, I tried to tell myself it was nothing. This couldn't be anything. Just a weird cyst or something.

The doctor spoke slowly, seriously, and in a low tone

as he asked me a battery of health questions. After the examination, the doctor explained the possibilities.

"Only one in ten of these is ever cancerous. It probably is an infection. We'll put you on antibiotics for two weeks."

My mouth was dry, my heart sank, and I nervously thanked him. As I walked down the narrow, dark hallway, I thought it has been too long for an infection. The receptionist smiled and said, "Good-bye". I put it out of my mind. It couldn't be cancer.

For those two weeks I faithfully took the antibiotics and quietly prayed that it would not be anything serious. After all, the doctor said it was only a one in ten chance. I was young, healthy, and a dedicated Christian.

It just wouldn't go away. When Alison asked me if I was better, seeing the concern in her eyes, I would say "Maybe!" But the lump, that pocket of potential death, was still there.

After two weeks the doctor said that he would have to do a biopsy of the testicle. He didn't believe it was cancer, but if it was, the safest way to biopsy was to remove the diseased testicle.

Whoa, I thought! This is too heavy and too fast. Now I felt that my manhood was involved.

The doctor assured me that I would still do all the things that men do without problems. But it made my gut ache to think about it.

Seven months had gone by since I first felt the lump. Now I was on my way to the hospital. As I looked at the green grass and blue sky, I felt that all would be okay on this sunny day. As the gentle breeze petted my face, I wondered if these days would change my life or would I be back to normal in a few days?

Pulling a razor blade from a cellophane package,

the EMT began to prepare for this outpatient surgery. We laughed about the process. Then he asked, "What kind of surgery are you having?" When I told him, I detected a look of horror in his eyes though he tried to cover it. Attempting to reassure him, I said, "The doctor says it was probably nothing. I'll be all right." But really I wanted to comfort myself. I didn't want to think about losing a testicle, let alone the possibility of cancer!

As they wheeled me into the operating room, my eyes were on Alison and my heart was on the Lord. Nervously she laughed and reminded me that she would be waiting. Our associate pastor prayed with us, and then I was whisked away through the large oak door.

The IV was plunged into my arm. As I moved my arm to adjust the IV, I noticed the nurse looked concerned. Now it was time to find out the truth. As the anesthesiologist opened the IV drip, I counted backwards, <u>100, 99, 98</u> ....

"Let me get you a blanket. You look cold." The nurse moved into sight and I realized that I was already in recovery. It was done and over. My lower abdomen felt like it had been beaten by Mohammed Ali. The nurse gave me ice for my parched and thirsty lips, then whisked me off to my room.

When Dr. Koerner, my urologist, came into the room, my heart began to race. Alison, Jack, our associate pastor, and I all nervously awaited his report. Taking his glasses off and raising his eyes from the charts, Dr. Koerner said that all went well. Based on his experience, the tumor did not look cancerous. I felt a release of tension. Great! I'll just go home, heal from surgery, and get back to work.

...Three days later the phone rang. Alison came into the room and said that Dr. Koerner's office had called. They needed to see me first thing Friday morning.

Why? What was the urgency?

...Now sitting in the doctor's office, the heartbreaking news.

"I'm sorry to tell you this, but the report of the biopsy shows that the tumor we removed five days ago was malignant and has probably spread to your lymph system. Without a cure, you will die within two years."

As we walked out of the doctor's office to get x-rays from the hospital, my whole body went numb. It seemed like time stood still. I was in a slow motion movie.

A million thoughts began to race through my mind. How can this be? I immediately turned to Alison and thought, "Who will take care of my family?" As my life flashed before my eyes I asked myself, "What if treatment doesn't work? Will I survive surgery? Can I ever be normal after all of this?" There was a lump in my throat and I felt alone, abandoned, and forsaken. We were in shock! This could not be true.

Chapter Two

THE VALLEY OF FEAR

How could he say that? It couldn't be right! Did I really hear him?

That one hour visit to the doctor turned into an eternity. So many questions had to be asked. A multitude of details needed to be covered. He had made a statement I did not want to accept.

According to the doctor, if the treatment was successful, my life would be put **ON HOLD** for a period of a year. There would be no time or strength to do the things that seemed important to me. Everything would have to wait. My life was about to center around doctors, hospitals, tests, and the moment by moment effort to get better.

After that time, provided there was no recurrence, my life could resume to normal.

It was Friday morning and the doctor wanted me in Indianapolis on Monday morning to undergo surgery. He acted as if there was no time to lose. It was imperative that we move quickly.

But how could I just drop everything, put my dreams, goals, responsibilities, and life **ON HOLD?** Fear, that nagging feeling, that gripping force, that paralyzing spirit grabbed my mind and began to strangle me. I couldn't figure it out. All of the sudden nothing made any sense!

Surgery seemed like the last thing on my agenda. It lurked at me like a monster from a horror movie, laughing and mocking, as it moved in for the kill.

There are a few things that I fear. Probably my number one fear is bumble bees. I just don't like those little bugs near me at all.

15

I remember driving on the Ohio Turnpike by myself when, without warning, there it was. That's right! A wasp had managed to come in on the last stop. It was whizzing about my head, circling for the kill. I could tell that it had a stinger with my name written on it. It wanted blood!

The traffic was bumper to bumper, 70 miles per hour. That didn't matter at all. With one poetic motion, the car skidded to a halt on a bridge, my body flew out of the vehicle with cars careening by. I found myself standing outside the car, nearly killed from traffic, but safe from the ominous danger of that wasp.

Boy, did I feel foolish. There I was in the middle of the turnpike. The wasp was still in the car! Fear!

I have an equal fear of shots. I panicked at the thought of a needle jabbing my skin, puncturing the tissue, and probing for a blood vessel. This terrified me!

Once, to avoid a tetanus shot, I asked the doctor to cauterize a puncture in my foot. I had stepped on a rusty nail. He must have had a sense of humor because when he swabbed it with alcohol, he said that it would hurt a little. Then he proceeded to apply the silver nitrate (gun powder)! Wow, I had never felt pain like that. The burning sensation began in the foot and took over my body. Without warning, I lost my breath, the room began to spin, and I had to lie down before I passed out.

Then I heard the voice of the Lord in my heart say, "You should have taken the tetanus shot." Fear! I had reacted in fear instead of responding in faith. Now I paid for it.

So, the thought of going into the hospital, surgery, intravenous therapy, and all the trappings of cancer treatment absolutely freaked me out.

Fear for my family, my friends, my responsibilities in the ministry, and for my life were all around me. I feared for my wife who would feel the many responsibilities of the household, much pressure would be on her shoulders. Surely, it's true that Dads Don't Die! To think that my son and daughter would change schools without the strength and availability of a father to guide them. I couldn't understand how the church would be pastored and the work continue if I was in such a condition. I didn't understand how it would work out, but I tried to tell myself that the Lord had everything under control. It would be all right.

Everyone battles fear at sometime. For some, the grip of fear is so oppressive that it contracts their every thought, decision, emotion, and experience.

The wise man said in the proverbs:

"Be not afraid of sudden fear, neither of the desolation of the wicked, when it cometh."
Proverbs 3:25(KJV)

It is interesting that the Bible says that the righteous will experience sudden fear, but the wicked experience desolation.

You cannot prevent the human responses of terror, fear, anxiety, apprehension, horror, fright, and dread. It is not a sign of weakness, but an indication of your humanity. The righteous feels this, but the wicked are destroyed.

In the darkness of cancer, the Lord delivered me from my fears. What follows are the truths that brought victory to me as I battled fear.

I. Fear is a Friend

When our daughter was young, she laid her hand on a hot stove. I remember the silence that was like the calm before the storm. Then suddenly the silence was broken with a bloodcurdling scream that sounded like a police siren. The pain was intense and I felt sorry for her.

After that, Sarah knew the danger of the stove. It produced in her a healthy fear. Now she would remember before she placed those tiny fingers near that stove. She knew the potential for hurt and suffering. Her fear was a friend.

The Bible speaks often of the fear of the Lord. The word does mean reverence and respect for God, but it also means healthy fear. Since God created you, you are accountable to Him. This is wonderful when we have done His will and pleased Him. It is stressful when we have disobeyed.

Paul, the Apostle spoke of this friendly fear:

"For we must all appear before the judgment seat of Christ, that each one may receive the things {done} in the body, according to what he has done, whether good or bad."
"Knowing, therefore, the terror of the Lord, we persuade men; but we are well known to God, and I also trust are well known in your consciences."
2 Corinthians 5:10-11

Paul was moved with fear when he realized the imminent situation of eternity and his day of accounting. It possessed him with a healthy fear that caused him to make good decisions and to set right priorities. You can only take into eternity that which you have done for Jesus Christ.

This kind of fear brings wonderful results. Look at its effects in the early church. (Acts 9:31)

This attitude and phobia produced a healthy climate that brought God's blessing in the Early Church. I remember when I became rebellious as a teen. I didn't want

18

to obey my parents. As a result, they spent many sleepless nights wondering where I was and what they could do to help me bring my life under control.

I didn't feel like I could ask them for anything because I was aware of the hurt I was causing them. I became arrogant and acted like I didn't need them.

At age sixteen, I gave my heart to Jesus Christ. I knew that I was saved and had a home in heaven. Obviously it had nothing to do with my good works, but the Lord graciously gave me the gift of salvation. I became so thankful for this undeserved gift that I wanted to please the Lord with my heart and lifestyle.

Now, the fear of displeasing the Lord, caused me to do what I wouldn't do before. I wanted to please my parents because I knew that it would please the Lord. This fear became my friend and created an atmosphere of blessing. I felt free to talk to my dad and mom about my needs. They were anxious to talk and to help.

This fear is a main ingredient in life for favor from both God and man.

Fear signals danger, and helps us to know how to make good and productive decisions in life.

II. Fear is a Foe

"The fear of man brings a snare, but whoever trusts in the Lord shall be safe." Proverbs 29:25 (NKJ)

Fear has a negative and devastating side. It can grab until we make poor decisions. I remember when people in the church began to resist my leadership. I was tempted to react in my fear. I feared rejection and thought that my priority should be to please those that were upset. Then I feared embarrassment and wanted to quit and run. After that came the fear of disaster. I wanted to die! I am glad that my Bishop gave me wise counsel during that time. He cautioned me against making any decisions under pressure. I must wait on the Lord to show me His will. Am I glad that I did. When I stayed in the will of God, the Lord worked everything out for my good.

Within a year the church was growing more than ever. The result was that the crowds became so big that we needed to build again. This produced a new wave of people that gave their lives to Jesus Christ and became some of the most wonderful friends and workers we have ever known.

When my treatments were over from the cancer, I faced many problems. Medical bills were piled high. My income was down. Our house sat half finished. We didn't have the money to tie up the loose ends. I wanted to sell the house and walk away. I feared that people would see me as a failure. I feared the bill collectors and public opinion.

Again, the counsel to me was to be patient. Don't make a decision under pressure. Give it six months and see what the Lord will do for you.

The fear of man was about to deprive me of what God wanted to do in my life. Within six months, all the bills were paid and the bank refinanced the house. This allowed us to finish our house. The offerings increased to provide adequate income. God is faithful.

The fear of man is a snare. When you react to fear that is based on the intimidations of man and circumstances, it will snare you into destruction.

III. Fear is in Opposition to Faith

Our first reaction to bad news is fear. This was just as true of the men of God in the Bible. Often Jesus would arrive on a scene and immediately minister to the fears of the disciples.

> *"But the ship was now in the midst of the sea, tossed with waves: for the wind was contrary."* *"And in the fourth watch of the night Jesus went unto them, walking on the sea."* *"And when the disciples saw him walking on the sea, they were troubled, saying, It is a spirit; and they cried out for fear."* *"But straightway Jesus spake unto them, saying, Be of good cheer; it is I; be not afraid."* *Matthew 14:24-27; 17:6-7* *"And when he had so said, he shewed unto them {his} hands and his side. Then were the disciples glad, when they saw the Lord."* *"Then said Jesus to them again, Peace {be} unto you: as {my} Father hath sent me, even so send I you."* *John 20:20-21*

In each of these incidences the disciples were filled with fear. Jesus knew that before He could do anything else for them, He had to minister to their fears. Why? Because fear opposes faith. Faith is the substance that pleases God and releases His laws and principles to work in our lives. It is impossible to walk in fear and faith at the same time. You must let go of one to embrace the other.

IV. Fear is Finished

> *"Yea, though I walk through the valley of the shadow of death, I will fear no evil: for thou {art} with me; thy rod and thy staff they comfort me."* *"Thou preparest a table before me in the presence of mine enemies: thou anointest my head with oil; my cup Runneth over."* *"Surely goodness and mercy shall follow me all the days of my life: and I will dwell in the house of the Lord for ever."* *Psalm 23:4-6*

Fear is finished because there is One who is greater than all of our fears that is well able to manage every need and circumstance. David learned this as a boy tending his father's sheep. He wrote this Psalm.

"The Lord {is} my shepherd; I shall not want." "He maketh me to lie down in green pastures: he leadeth me beside the still waters." "He restoreth my soul: he leadeth me in the paths of righteousness for his name's sake." "Yea, though I walk through the valley of the shadow of death, I will fear no evil: for thou {art} with me; thy rod and thy staff they comfort me." Psalm 23

That is why he could face a Goliath.

You and God make a majority. The writer in Hebrews conveys the same thought.

"{Let your} conversation {be} without covetousness; {and be} content with such things as ye have: for he hath said, I will never leave thee, nor forsake thee." "So that we may boldly say, The Lord {is} my helper, and I will not fear what man shall do unto me." Hebrews 13:5-6

The good news is that fear is now conquered because Jesus Christ has won every battle. Even death is defeated in the Lord Jesus Christ.

"Forasmuch then as the children are partakers of flesh and blood, he also himself likewise took part of the same; that through death he might destroy him that had the power of death, that is, the devil;" "And deliver them who through fear of death were all their lifetime subject to bondage." Hebrews 2:14-15

When you have the Lord in your life you receive a great advantage over fear. There is an awareness that the Lord is above, around, under, and in you. That means no evil thing can touch you without His permission. If He allows it, it is for your good. God only wants what is best for you. His plan for your life is to accomplish His purposes in us!

God loves you. All that He does and allows is for your good. The love of God has the power to extract all fear and replace it with peace and confidence. We can trust Him!

Chapter Three

THE VALLEY OF DENIAL!

It was a cold wintery day in the south of England in February of 1986.   Sixty days after I first detected the unwanted addition to my testicle, Alison and I were in Ashford of Kent to attend and speak at a church growth conference with our friends.   Unwilling to face my condition, I had not yet consulted a doctor.

As we walked from the hotel to the church building with the cold morning air wisping across our faces, we were stopped by our good friend, Pastor Willie Bolden.

This talented African-American man always had a joyful spirit and had an ability to communicate the Gospel in a way that moved hearts tremendously.   This morning, though, he seemed a little fidgety and upset.

He pulled me aside.   I noticed that he was looking down towards the ground.   It was hard for him to look me straight in the eye.   I knew that he was concerned about something.

"Rod," he said, "I've needed to talk to you.   Last night, I had a dream about you."

"In that dream, I saw death like a blackness running through your body."   He said, "All the details are not important, but I dreamed this dream several times through the night and always the same death like blackness was running through your body."

Stepping toward the curb to cross the street, he looked me straight in the face and with a serious stare, said, "I felt the Lord wanted me to let you know that it is imperative that you get to the doctor and be checked as soon as possible."

Pastor Bolden had no way of knowing what I was

going through during that time. Since November of 1985, a lump had formed and was growing on my right testes. I tried to pass it off as nothing. I kept telling myself that it would go away. I was hoping that the Lord would touch me and heal me so that I wouldn't have to deal with it. But it was still there and now supernaturally, miraculously God was letting me know that He wanted me to take care of myself.

The summer after treatments Pastor Bolden and I played a round of golf together. I was still weak from my chemotherapy, but had begun to feel like a normal person again. As he swung his club, grinned with a winsomical look in his eyes, and jested about the game, I found myself thanking the Lord for the miracle of revelation. What would have happened if he had not been faithful to share his dream and the word he felt that he had heard from God.

It's strange that as human beings we often deny the reality of our condition. Those that work with cancer now tell us one of the keys to a cure for most cancers is early detection and early treatment. Yet, even though I knew that, I did not want to own the reality of my situation, so I kept with life in a "business as usual" fashion.

You see this problem of denial in so many areas. As a pastor, often I see it in grief. I think about the many wives, children, and husbands that I have stood with when somebody that they have loved has passed away. And often you hear them say, "I just can't believe this has happened."

Denial is a part of our human nature, but it is a weakness that can produce dangerous consequences.

We tend to change our viewpoint of reality every time a new trend moves on the scene, or television tells us things are different, or our mood swings.

Consequently, we have been an escapist generation looking for a way out of our painful circumstances. This is called denial.

That's where I was. I was denying my condition. It was real. It was happening and I needed to do something about it.

Help was available. Something could be done, but not until I was willing to acknowledge that I had a problem and I needed help.

The biggest problem that people face is the resistance to acknowledge their problem. God is a great God who is able to help us in many ways, but not until we are willing to admit the reality of the situation and are willing to seek help.

Pride is the downfall of mankind.

"{When} pride cometh, then cometh shame: but with the lowly {is} wisdom." Proverbs 11:2
"Only by pride cometh contention but with the well advised {is} wisdom." Proverbs 13:10
"A man's pride shall bring him low: but honour shall uphold the humble in spirit." Proverbs 29:23
"Pride {goeth} before destruction, and an haughty spirit before a fall." Proverbs 16:18

Sin translates into a self-centered mentality. It is a mentality that says all I need is me. I can do it, I can take care of myself. I don't need anybody else or anything else.

The one thing that separates people from God, His presence, and His provision in our lives is self. Self-centeredness, self-pity, self-dependence, and self-righteousness will destroy us!

Even though I was a Christian and understood that principle from the Scripture, I found that self was subtly moving in on the scene. It wanted to keep me from receiving the help that God intended for me to have.

But now, with a whipping wind on my cheeks and

snowflakes filtering through the air and landing on my nose, eyes and cheeks, I was hearing a message from God. Don't deny your situation. There is help available. Do something about it.

If we will admit our situation, then we can do something about it. The only people who never get any help are the people who never look for help. Jesus taught us if we will seek, we will find. If we knock, the door will be opened to us. If we ask, we shall receive. (Matthew 7:7-8)

Help may not always come in the way that we want it to come, but God always answers every prayer. God will answer every prayer in one of three ways. He will either say "yes," "no," or "wait".

In this situation, God's yes was already there, but I needed to do something about it. God does answer prayer, but we must cooperate with His answers. We have to do something for Him to work in our lives.

I mustered the biggest smile I knew how and said to Pastor Bolden, "Thank you for your faithfulness. I can't explain right now what that means, but I want you to know, I understand what you are saying. I will go to the doctor as soon as I can when I get back."

What would the doctors say? How would it affect my life? Was the Lord preparing to take me home? I am only thirty-two years old, can this be for real? How will the kids feel, my parents react, the church respond?

If it isn't cancer, then what? As I walked with Alison and saw her smile, I wondered if I would be around for another Christmas or birthday? More than that, I began to wonder if my life had meant anything significant to God? If I did die, what would He say of my efforts and my heart?

As I left England, I had taken a step forward. Denial was behind me. Now, though it was hard to do, I knew I had to go and find the answers to my problem. I now knew that denial was a prison that would rob me of the very opportunities that God was preparing for me. My mind was made up, I would do whatever I had to. By God's help I was ready to face it, grace it, and erase it from my life.

DESTROYING SELF-DECEPTION

Since denial plagues our society and is such a part of our human nature, I have had to ask myself, "How can I fight against denial in my life?" I am convinced that there is victory available, so how does God help us to be free from deception, especially self-deception? Let me suggest three things the Lord has shown me in the Bible.

1) Inventory Yourself Daily

"If we confess our sins, he is faithful and just to forgive us our sins, and to cleanse us from all unrighteousness."   I John 1:9

The Lord has taught us He is a gracious and forgiving God. However, His forgiveness is based on our willingness to confess our sin. This confession requires inventory.

Jesus said that when the Holy Spirit would come, that He would convict us of sin.

"And when He is come, he will convict the world of sin, and of righteousness, and of judgment:"
John 16:8

This word "convict" is an old King James word that means to convince us. The Holy Spirit, who is a person, comes to us to help us recognize our weakness, difficulty, and guilt before society, ourselves and God. He is faithful to make sin real to us.

His ministry is not effective, though, until we respond with a "confession". The word "confession" in the Greek means to agree in one word. In other words, God just wants us to agree with Him about our condition. When we are willing to agree with Him and repent of that condition, the Lord forgives us.

The word "repent" is another old English word that simply means to change your mind or to turn around. I am walking in one direction and now I do an about face. I turn around and walk the other direction.

As long as we live in denial, no repentance can happen. It is only when we are willing to acknowledge our situation for what it is that we can turn around. But when we turn around, forgiveness, grace, and help is available to us.

2) Intimately Relate to Others

"as iron sharpeneth iron; so a man sharpeneth the countenance of his friend." Proverbs 27:17

It is very important, in order to be free from self-deception and denial, that we establish relationships with people that can be transparent.

In I Corinthians 15:33, the Bible says:

"Be not deceived: Evil company corrupts good morals."

You may have a good attitude, but all it takes to develop a bad attitude is to link up with the wrong people. This is a part of the denial system that we fight day by day, especially in today's society. When we don't like the truth that we hear from someone, be it a friend, pastor, or church, our first tendency is to run to another group that will agree with our position. This is not the work of the Holy Spirit.

I have noticed in my own life that I struggle with a tendency to blame others for my situation. Have you ever had the problem that you know in your heart you are wrong, but you want to look good to other people? So instead, you say those things that make you look good and justify your weakness and your problems. That is another form of denial.

This is why it is so important to find trusted relationships that can be transparent and honest with you. They should never take the place of the Holy Spirit in your life, but it is good to have someone who can look you in the face and simply say, "I'm not sure I agree with that" or "Doesn't the Bible say".

That is why I thank the Lord for men who are sensitive and honest like Pastor Bolden. He didn't tell me everything would be okay. That came later. He knew from the Lord the urgency to say that it was time to do something about my problem.

3) Identify with Human Weakness

People tend to live their lives with the thought that these circumstances only happen to other people. Everyone else experiences tragedy. Everyone else goes through difficulty, but I am not going to face this trouble.

I felt that this couldn't be happening to me because I am only thirty-two years old, love God and serve Jesus Christ. This couldn't be happening to me because these things only happen to other people that I visit in the hospital and nursing home. But they don't touch me or my family.

I don't suggest that we become morbid with this thought, because we can become so internalized that we paralyze ourselves. Yet, there is a need to understand that all of us are vulnerable. Even Job, whom God said was a righteous man, felt the pain and torment of death, poverty, weakness, loss, and depression. God did help him.

Admitting a need to ourselves and God brings amazing results. When we are self-sufficient and invulnerable, those who would help can't. Confessing that we are weak and needy creates the opportunity for help to arrive.

God who is full of grace and love wants to help, but He will not help us if we are in denial. He requires that we be honest with ourselves and with Him. Then help will be available.

4) Invite God to Help You

Perhaps you find yourself in denial as you read this book. God loves you and wants to help you. I found that when I was willing to admit to myself my condition and humble myself to the Lord, He was ready and willing to help me. What He has done for me, He will do for you. We have to fight against "DENIAL".

Jesus Christ made an incredible invitation to everyone in the book of Revelation in the Bible.

"Behold, I stand at the door and knock. If anyone hears My voice and opens the door, I will come in to him and dine with him, and he with Me."
Revelation 3:20

God's love for all of us is so great that it is hard for us to humanly comprehend it. The greatest picture of that love is seen in what He did for us in history.

"For God so loved the world that He gave His only begotten Son, that whoever believes in Him should not perish but have everlasting life. For God did not send His Son into the world to condemn the world, but that the world through Him might be saved. He who believes in Him is not condemned; but he who does not believe is condemned already, because he has not believed in the name of the only begotten Son of God."
John 3:16-18

That is real love! As a father, I cannot imagine asking my son to die for another. Yet what I would not want to do, God did for me and for all people of all time. In His death on the cross, Jesus Christ provided the means of forgiveness from God and the gift of eternal life.

The simplicity of this plan makes it difficult for many. God wanted everyone to be able to receive this gift of life, no matter what their race, nationality, physical condition, mental ability, or place in life may be. That is why Jesus said that we must become as a child to enter into the Kingdom of Heaven. God requires only one thing, simple child-like faith in His promise and provision to give us eternal life.

Jesus promised that He would live in us. But He is the perfect gentleman and He will never force Himself on us. That is why He said that if we hear His voice and open the door, we will receive this new life and special relationship. If you have never asked Christ to come into your life, let me encourage you to do so. Jesus Christ is where you are today. If you feel a tug on your heart, I urge you to respond to Him and invite Him into your life through this simple prayer.

Dear Lord Jesus Christ,

Thank you for loving me and dying for me. I believe that you are risen from the dead and in this place. I confess my weakness, faults, and shortcomings. I thank you that I am already forgiven through your death on the cross. I invite you to live in me and to take control of my life. Please use my life to bring honor to you. Thank you for hearing this prayer. Amen!

If you prayed that prayer, then it has happened. God cannot lie and He would not lie to you. If you asked Him to come into your heart, then He is there. You will begin to see a difference. As you listen, you will hear His voice in your heart. When you read the Bible, you will understand it in a way you never did, because the Author is living in you.

This is a new life in you. It is like a seed that has been planted in your inner man. As you attend a church that teaches the Bible as God's Word, pray daily, read the Bible, and share this faith with others, this new life will grow in you.

If you are already a child of God, remember to ask for God's help. Denial and self-deception are destructive, but as you face your situation and invite God to help you, He will.

"Call to Me, and I will answer you, and show you great and mighty things, which you do not know." Jeremiah 33:3

Chapter Four

THE VALLEY OF THOUGHTS

Won't this hurt go away? My knees felt weak. My speech was uncontrolled. My thoughts were confused. I felt dizzy and faint.

I knew I needed to talk to those that I trusted to find help and guidance. So many decisions were thrust upon me in just a few moments of time. Now my whole life has changed.

It nagged at me as we drove away from the hospital and headed for our home. Alison and I didn't say much. The sun was shining and dancing on the hood of the car. The air was warm, but it didn't seem to be that way. I reached over to hold Alison's hand. I don't know if I wanted to console her or me. Either way it was comforting to know that she was there. We prayed. I knew that God was there, but why couldn't I get rid of this feeling of hopelessness, desperation, and distress.

That day was horrible. It is difficult to understand. It's like the panic you feel when you know your car is skidding on ice and you are headed for another car. You are in danger, out of control and you have no options. I heard one cancer patient describe it as "when the Mack truck hit her".

Each time I told someone else the circumstance, the despair, anguish, and sadness would overwhelm me. I sat in our pastor's office. My desire was to be dignified, to look good, to say with an air of confidence that I could handle it. Instead, the tears began to stream down my cheeks and to roll off of my jaw. As I talked, I could feel my shirt moistening from what seemed to be a river of tears.

It was uncomfortable to tell the story. I instantly sensed sympathy, concern, and hurt. "I don't want to be a burden. I don't like to make others uncomfortable," I said to myself. Yet, this situation did not affect me only. The responsibility was mine.

As we talked, I was overwhelmed with the importance of these loved ones to me. What if I didn't get better? I did not want to be a great burden. I wanted to be a blessing. Every thought intensified the pain.

The "what if's" were frightening. What if I recover but I am physically or mentally impaired? What if I die, but I die a slow torturous death as I had seen others do? What if my family, friends, and wife are forced to center their lives and finances on nursing me for years? What if I am sexually impaired?

It was embarrassing to have lost a testicle. I could hardly say the words when people asked what type of cancer I had. The thought of impotency was terrifying. That would be a failure of failures. What if no one cared and I was left alone?

I had to repeat the story several times that day. The staff needed to know. My daughter and son would have to be informed. I thought, "Wow, how can I tell them without frightening them? How can I say it and give them hope when I am raging on the inside? What if I'm not allowed to watch them grow up, graduate, get married?" But I received personal assurance. . . DADS DON'T DIE!

When I called my mother, I tried to be strong and just say it, but before I could finish the first sentence, tears started again, and my voice revealed the torment and fear that was a consuming fire in my emotions.

As I pulled myself together, I reassured my grieving, weeping mother that all would work out. God had everything under control, even though I didn't understand it.

After I hung up, I could tell that this was an unbearable burden on Alison. She hadn't said much. She was trying to be strong. We sat down on the couch together and held each other. We didn't want to let go. Reassurance lived in that embrace for both of us.

Telling the children was a little easier. Children seem to have that ability to believe that all will be fine without questions. They took it in stride and acted as if I would not die. Dads do not die.

Sitting on the couch by myself, I ended that first day trying to pray, but unable to sense any peace or strength. I was panicked, wearied, and exhausted. Lying down in bed next to Alison, aching in my groin from the surgery, pondering the future, I found it difficult to sleep. Finally, thank God, I dozed off.

The next morning, as the sun pierced through the beige curtains, a wonderful thing happened. If you believe in the supernatural you will understand what I am about to write. I felt God speak to me. It wasn't an audible voice, but that still and small voice spoke into my spirit.

"Finally, brethren, whatsoever things are true, whatsoever things {are} honest, whatsoever things {are} just, whatsoever things {are} pure, whatsoever things {are} lovely, whatsoever things {are} of good report; if {there be} any virtue, and if {there be} any praise, think on these things." Phillipians 4:8

I said, "Lord, what are you trying to say to me?" Then I heard His voice speak back, "If you will begin to think about what I'll do for you and through you in this circumstance, I'll take care of you. Everything will be all right."

That's when I made my choice. I decided, "I will

refuse to think in the negative realm of 'what if' and 'if only'. I will refuse the negative and begin to think about what I will do and what God will accomplish through this experience."

It was miraculous because when I made that decision, something incredible happened. I was filled with the most wonderful peace and confidence. It was so powerful, that it filled me that moment and stayed with me from that time on. It was the peace that passes all natural understanding. (Phillipians 4:7) God had touched me when I made a decision to think what was true, honest, pure, just, lovely, and of a good report.

Thoughts Determine Our Attitude, Emotion, and Direction

"For as he thinketh in his heart, so {is} he:"
Proverbs 23:7

I began to see that thoughts determine my attitude, emotion, and direction. This is a key to dealing with the big and small circumstances that arise in our lives.

Our thoughts have a dramatic effect. For example, the medical world now tells us that the majority of physical illnesses treated in America are not caused physically, but instead are psycho-symatically induced. The fears, guilt, lack of confidence, and a loss sense of worth move people into physical and emotional illnesses.

Our thoughts produce our character. That is the message of the wise man. As he thinketh in his heart so is he. Character is the sum total of decisions that a person makes in their lives. Decisions are based on our thoughts. So our thoughts determine our direction, attitude, and the kind of person we are and will be.

Every time I expressed my fears or guilt feelings without hope or faith, it cemented those thoughts in my consciousness and made them a part of me.

On the other hand, when I learned to express my pain and questions with a hope and faith statement, I made that hope and faith a part of me. So my thoughts determine my attitude, emotions, and direction.

It is important to know that the pain is real. The grief is not to be denied, and the questions are normal. It all needs to be expressed. I found that how I express it determines my state and future.

Life is filled with circumstances that we don't understand because we don't know everything. Because God is all wise, we can trust Him with life's ups and downs.

When our children were little they used to ask us the question, "Why?" We would try to answer these questions to the best of our ability. Some of the questions had to do with faith. Questions like, "Why does the moon revolve around the earth?" It could not be explained to a three year old child. Later they would understand.

Satan's Strongholds Are in Our Minds

"For though we walk in the flesh, we do not war according to the flesh." "For the weapons of our warfare {are} not carnal but mighty in God for pulling down strongholds," "casting down arguments and every high thing that exalts itself against the knowledge of God, bringing every thought into captivity to the obedience of Christ," 2 Corinthians 10:3-5

The strongholds described are thoughts and the patterns of thinking that develop. These thoughts can be used of the enemy to strangle the strength right out of us. Such thoughts deceive and cause us to feel negative and develop a defeated attitude, which results in poor decisions. Negative thoughts will send us in the wrong direction and make us the very people that we don't want to be.

When bad news comes, I have the tendency to jump to the worst of conclusions. Before that day was over, I had visualized myself in a casket with a mourning widow and discouraged children gathered around. What if dads DO die? If I had not overcome the control and consequences of those thoughts, they would have consumed me.

I may not see in my lifetime the fulfillment of the plan that God has in today's events, but God does. He sees from the beginning to the end.

It is not over until the Lord says it is over. He is in control of our lives. In our grief, we may not understand why, but we do know who holds our hands and is in charge of our lives. This is the blessed heritage of those who know and love Jesus Christ and live in His will. He sees the big picture. He will work every detail of life for our good according to His purpose.

> *"And we know that all things work together for good to them that love God, to them who are the called according to {his} purpose." "For whom he did foreknow, he also did predestinate {to be} conformed to the image of his Son, that he might be the firstborn among many brethren." Romans 8:28-29*

People feel a lump and they jump to conclusions. We forget that 80% of all lumps are non-malignant. Even when we know, that we still tend to think the worst. Don't borrow trouble. It's not over until it's over.

The doctor says that this is terminal and you will die

within so many months. Remember, God has the final word. I cooperated with my doctor in the process of treatment. But remember that Jesus Christ has declared Himself to be the one who holds the keys to death.

> *"I {am} He who lives, and was dead, and behold, I am alive forevermore. Amen. And I have the keys of Hades and of Death." Revelation 1:18*

Only He can allow your life to be taken. Until that time you can rest assured that God has a good plan for your life and circumstance. Hang in there. Look up because God knows something that you don't know.

Fear of Recurrence

One of the pressures of cancer is the threat of recurrence. You can't be sure if it is wiped out on a microscopic level. Often the nagging thought of "what if a recurrence" would try to haunt me. One day I was hassling with that, when the Lord spoke to my spirit two words, "No recurrence." That was it. I was able to hang on to that witness and fight away all of the fears and doubts that would try to possess me.

That may or may not be God's message to you. God works in each of us differently. The key is to hear in your heart that word that God is saying to you, then to stand on it.

> *"And they overcame him by the blood of the Lamb and by the word of their testimony, and they did not love their lives to the death." Revelation 12:11*

Speaking our testimony of the things that God has said are true gives us the strength to overcome our adversity.

Anything that God speaks to our hearts has to agree with what He has already written. God would never contradict Himself. If it doesn't harmonize with the Bible, then it cannot be true. True faith comes from hearing, and hearing the Word of God (Romans 10:17), not by what we feel or decide for ourselves. When we know that God says it, that settles it. Then real faith can operate.

Thoughts can determine an upward experience or they can push us down. You can be strengthened. Identify what you believe instead of your doubts. Identify the good things that are happening. As you talk of the true, honest, pure, just, lovely, and the things of a good report, you will sense that the peace of God will keep your heart.

Chapter Five

THE VALLEY WITH MIRACLES

"When we finish with you, you will feel like a truck has run over you. You will be as if 1,000 fighters have beat your body to pieces. You will not feel like you are even alive any more," dialogued the doctor.

As the doctor said these things to me, I looked towards Alison. On the outside she was smiling, but I knew deep down inside, she felt afraid--concerned about the future. At the same time, we both sensed that overwhelming peace of God. Four weeks earlier God had assured my heart that if I would keep my mind on Him, that He would take me through. Now His promise afforded us tremendous peace.

We gathered in a circle and held hands. Again I felt that wonderful peace of God.

Now lying there in a hospital gown with no back, I flipped through a magazine and ate my meal by myself. To pass the time I turned on the television. I was pleased to see that our home church, Calvary Temple of Fort Wayne, was on the broadcast that evening. Pastor Paul Craig was giving an appeal for those who needed a miracle in their life to stretch out their hand and to believe with them in faith that God could touch them.

I had one of those unusual experiences. As a pastor, I had sat in many meetings where such a prayer was given. Generally, I just exercised faith for others and occasionally asked God to touch me. This night everything felt different because on this night as the pastor spoke those words, "We are going to believe for a miracle", I sensed in my heart that

God was speaking right to me. It was time for me to believe for my miracle.

Sitting straight up in bed with my eyes intent on the eyes of the pastor, I stretched my hand out with him. As he closed his eyes and began to pray that the Lord would touch those who were releasing and expressing faith at that moment, I felt the power and glory of God rush into my room. If you have ever felt it, it is a wonderful thing. For when the Lord is present, you feel a warmth and a renewed sense of peace--an awesome awareness that He who created all things and controls all things is standing with you. Now I felt that presence in my room.

As the pastor said, "Amen," I, too, said, "Amen." Then I said, "Lord, I'm going to trust You. I don't understand all that I am going through, but I know that You are with me and I trust You." With that, I settled back in my bed and enjoyed the peace and joy that comes only from knowing the Lord. I was not worried about the surgery the next day. I knew whatever would happen, God was with me!

About an hour passed when unexpectedly my surgeon knocked on my door and entered the room. This white-haired urologist was in charge of all the research and surgery for the medical center in the area of testicular cancer. I could tell immediately that he had several things on his mind.

Shuffling his feet he made a note on his clipboard, looked up and held it tight to his chest, putting a wrinkle in the white medical coat that he wore. He smiled at me and said, "Mr. Buzzard, we have a change in game plans." I asked, "Really, what do you mean?" He said, "Well, if you remember, it just so happened today, we gave you a routine chest x-ray." I replied, "I remember that." But in my mind I was saying to myself, "He used the words, 'It just so happens'." You know when you are a child of God, those words always cause those antennas to go up. In God's economy there are no coincidences. The steps of a righteous man are ordered of the Lord. Immediately it caught my attention.

The doctor went on to say, "It just so happens that the world's leading pulmonary radiologist, from Germany, is in the hospital for these three weeks." I got a little more excited. Then he said, "It just so happens that when your x-rays were on the wall, he walked into the viewing room." Now I was on the edge of my bed. Then he said, "And it just so happens that he took an interest in your x-rays. It just so happens that when he reviewed your x-rays, he saw a small nodule of cancer, no larger than the end of your small finger, in the lower left quadrant of your lung, about here." He pointed to his chest with his pencil.

"So," he said, "that presents a whole new circumstance. As a result of his keen and perceptive eye, we know everything we wanted to know from that surgery. This means that you will **NOT** have to be in eight to ten hours of surgery dissecting those lymph nodes. It also means that you won't have to recover here in the hospital for a week, nor will you have to spend the next weeks in recovery at home only to return to the hospital and begin treatments of chemotherapy."

"Tomorrow we will have the doctors and their medical team meet with you so that you can immediately begin your treatments of chemotherapy."

I was absolutely beside myself. No one was there for me to share this with, except the Lord. I knew in my heart that the miracle that had been witnessed in my spirit just moments before was now being reported to me. God had spared me the agony of that surgery.

The next day when I met with the medical team, they

began to describe to me the treatment that would be involved. As the doctor reviewed my charts and discussed my case, he commented to me that because we had caught the cancer in this early state, there was tremendous hope. This one cancer was the most treatable of all cancers. Their overall success rate was 95%.

Another doctor explained, "Pastor Buzzard, we want to encourage you because this means that your chances of cure are in the 99 percentile range. One of the reasons this has happened is because you didn't have the surgery and we will be able to start the chemotherapy right away. This lack of delay has improved your chances of cure dramatically and will help you to recover from the chemotherapy more quickly. You can really be thankful that the x-rays caught this at this point in time."

All of a sudden that phrase, "it just so happens", became a beacon of hope in my mind. Now I not only knew in my spirit, but I could see in my circumstance that God was with me and helping me. There is no greater joy and no more wonderful sense of security than to know that the Lord is with you in the midst of difficulty.

Some might argue whether or not it was just coincidence. The Holy Spirit strengthens my faith to believe that God spoke to an angel who put his hand on that radiologist. It was God's perfect time. God had moved into that room and emphasized and magnified that x-ray to the doctor. This improved my chances for recovery and spared me from that surgery.

I could not believe it. As a child of God, there aren't any "accidents", only divine arrangements. All of a sudden I was aware that God had made an arrangement for me. He had a plan!

God can and does cause everything to work for our good.

"And he that searcheth the hearts knoweth what {is} the mind of the Spirit, because he maketh intercession for the saints according to {the will of} God...." *"Moreover whom he did predestinate, them he also called: and whom he called, them he also justified: and whom he justified, them he also glorified."* *"What shall we then say to these things? If God {be} for us, who {can be} against us?"* Romans 8:27; 30-31

We may not understand how, but He sees from the beginning to the end and has a plan. If we live according to His purpose, the Lord makes a way to turn tragedy into triumph. That day I knew that I was a direct recipient of His plan, His care and His love!

Another example of this divine arrangement was in the chemotherapy that was used as a cure. The likelihood of the chemicals being tested on testicular cancer was one in billions. Yet, the researchers came upon the information that led them to believe that it should be tested. A cure was found!

A few years later I met Dr. Einhorn. He is an unassuming man. I said to him, "It is a real pleasure and privilege to meet the man who discovered this cure." He just smiled and said, "All of us get lucky sometime."

But I knew that it was more than luck, it was divine intervention for my life. This left me with an awesome awareness of God's ability to minister and to provide. As I read my Bible during those days I was reminded of the story of Abraham. God asked Abraham to take his son to Mt. Moriah to sacrifice him. Abraham bravely obeyed.

"And Abraham stretched forth his hand, and took the knife to slay his son. And the angel of the Lord called unto him out of heaven, and said, Abraham,

---

Abraham: and he said, Here {am} I. And Abraham lifted up his eyes, and looked, and behold behind {him} a ram caught in a thicket by his horns: and Abraham went and took the ram, and offered him up for a burnt offering in the stead of his son. And Abraham called the name of that place Jehovahjireh: as it is said {to} this day, In the mount of the Lord it shall be seen." Genesis 22:10-14

The name of the place was called "Jehovahjireh" which means "the LORD sees" and "the LORD provides". In this I found several comforting truths.

* God does permit us to be tested. It is just a test.
* God sees our needs before we do and has a plan as it relates to His purpose and our good.
* God is able to provide every single need.
* If we obey Him, He does provide.

If you find yourself in difficulty today, I encourage you to relax and trust God. Your situation is only a test. It is not there to destroy you. God saw you and your situation before you were born and has the ability to provide all that you will ever need according to His plan and purpose. As you surrender to Him, He will provide an answer for you.

Chapter Six

THE VALLEY WITH FRIENDS

"You will feel as if you had the flu one hundred times over. Within a few weeks your hair will fall out. There is no question about it. You will lose it on your head, your face, and everywhere you have hair on your body. You will become so sick that you will begin to lose weight because you will not be able to eat for several weeks. The treatment we are to give you is chemotherapy in industrial doses. If you weren't a young man, this treatment alone would kill you. But because you are young, you will survive it and in time, your body will snap back," the doctor "reassured" me.

I thought what could be worse than surgery. Then I found out the answer..."chemotherapy".

The doctor went on to tell me that I would become sick in the next few weeks. Because of that, he wanted to accompany my "chemo" treatments with heavy doses of tranquilizers. Some of those medications he said would cause me to have amnesia. That meant once the treatments started until they ended, I would lose most of my short-term memory for a period of time.

To this day I have little memory of being in the hospital once the treatments began. But I do remember the effects.

As they wheeled the IV's in for the first series of treatments, I became anxious at the thought of being punctured again. I was thankful to see that there were many friends standing around me. It was those friends that really made a difference in my life during that time.

"Now you need to lie still because the effects of this

will start within a few minutes. Once the tranquilizers kick in, you will not have the control of your mind that you like to have."

The IV's were set and the poisons, cisplatin and VP-16, along with sedatives began to flow. Within minutes of the flow of that IV, I began to feel the queasy effects on my stomach. It was more than just a discomfort. Within a couple hours, it became a wrenching, violent evil in my body. The only way that I can describe it is, it must be like purposely drinking "Drano" and the effects that it would have as it hit your organs.

With that first blast, doubling over from my stomach being twisted by the chemicals, I found great comfort again in seeing my friends standing about me.

Four weeks later I lay in the hospital bed. Suffering from a septic infection, they rushed me to emergency, admitted me for intravenous, antibiotic treatments. My white blood count was so low that if I did not receive the medication, I would die.

By this time I felt like I had lost all control of my life. I couldn't do what I liked to do, I didn't have the strength. I couldn't eat what I wanted to eat, the vomiting had continued for weeks. Mashed potatoes and jello were the most that I could handle. I couldn't read, carry on long conversations, or even pray because my mind would not focus.

Now I felt angry. I was tired of being poked, dressed in hospital gowns with a slit up my back, and told where I could go and what I could do. I knew that I was only one third of the way through the treatment. I wondered if it could get any worse. It did!

As Alison came in that morning, I sat up on the hospital bed. The room was alive from the late July sun that revealed the off white walls, pure white sheets and yellow blanket, and the chrome railing on the bed. Then I noticed that covering the blankets was hair. Not just a few strands, but an abnormally big amount. Looking at the white speckled tile, I noticed more hair. I thought, "It can't all be mine." I had hoped that the doctor's prophecy wouldn't come true.

After showering, I began to dry my hair. As I spread my fingers to comb my hair with my hands, I felt a clump of hair stick in the wedge of my fingers. Looking down at my hand, I saw a huge lock of hair. Within a few minutes almost half of my hair fell out on the sterile bathroom floor of that hospital.

That week, it all fell out. But it did not stop with my head. I lost my eyebrows, facial hair, arm hair, and anywhere else that it grew... It was gone and I felt and looked like a freak. I was embarrassed. I was concerned about making others feel uncomfortable.

That first week I wore an Indiana Jones style hat to attempt to hide the effects of the treatments. Of course, any thing I did could not cover what was obviously unnatural. I went to church that Sunday. They released me from the hospital for the weekend. I was to re-enter the next week for more chemotherapy.

As I sat on the platform, the church was moved to tears. I didn't want that because I desired to see the people uplifted, not depressed. I began to wonder if I should have even gone to the service.

Bald, looking malnourished, weak, and anemically discolored in my skin (it looked a pale green), I couldn't make it on my own. Each week the effects of the chemotherapy cumulated. That means that the side effects multiplied. I was happy to think there was a cure, but I couldn't endure the misery and pain that was involved.

As I moved into the second course of treatment, my condition deteriorated with each day. It was all that I could do to move from the bedroom to the living room downstairs in the morning. I couldn't even watch television for long, because the effort would weaken me and I would begin to black out.

God used my friends and family to strengthen and carry me. Alison was right at my side throughout the summer. She would not leave unless it was necessary. Daily she attempted to comfort me, though often I could not be comforted by anything.

I remember that on several occasions she would ask me if I wanted to eat. I was always hungry and so I said that I did. She would faithfully prepare something, only to have me take a bite, and then become nauseated by the smell and taste (Alison is a gourmet cook) and have her take it away.

For hours she would sit and read across the room. She wanted to talk, but I couldn't. Yet, I hated to be alone. At that point, I just want the encouragement that came from familiar company.

At night I couldn't relax if someone was touching me. It was a feeling of being totally bruised and beaten till it hurt to be touched. It became so bad that for many weeks I would ask Alison to sleep in our daughter's bedroom.

Along with Alison, Joshua and Sarah became more important to me than anything in this world. Just to hear them say, "Hi, Dad", or "I love you, Dad", and "I'm praying for you, Dad" produced strength and joy. I can't say enough about the importance of these best friends that are mine.

My mom and dad were fabulous. Our relationship was strengthened. One afternoon I was very emotional from the tranquilizers and the events. There was anxiety over schedules and details surrounding my care and treatment. I was at the end of my rope. I had peace that God was with me, but I was feeling alone. Dad was so good. He just sat down on the couch and put his arm around me to console me for over an hour. They watched our children, mowed the grass and bought us a new bed.

Along with my immediate family, I have an extended family, the church. All of the wonderful people at Calvary Chapel of Auburn were such a tremendous help, that words are not sufficient to express my appreciation.

Day after day they poured over us with love. Daily we received cards, letters, visits, or a knock on the door to say, "We know Pastor doesn't feel well, but we brought you and the family something to eat." Their affection and prayers were the agencies of strength and healing that I needed.

I can't emphasize enough the importance of relationships. When I was sick, that was all that I had. Cars, homes, clothing, position, money, popularity, or recognition did not matter. All that counted were those that I loved.

As a pastor, I was blessed with other ministers that rushed to my aid at that time.

Dennis Kutzner was the executive secretary of our fellowship of churches called Calvary Ministries, Inc. International. Through his efforts, the office was maintained, pulpit filled with pastors who left their churches to help, and the peoples' needs were met in my absence.

One day Dennis came by to visit me. I had been especially sick that day. When Dennis arrived, I was on my hands and knees in the bathroom with my head hanging over the toilet. I had been so sick that day that the vomiting came every couple of minutes. Weakened by the constant movement back and forth from my easy chair to the washroom, I finally decided to just stay there and wait for the next convulsive eruption.

Seeing Dennis in the entry way, I called to Alison to

shut the door. He didn't need to see me that way. As the pine door began to sweep over the mauve carpet making a rubbing sound, I heard Dennis say, "Please, let me go in." Alison tried to stop him and I spoke out that it wasn't necessary, I wasn't good company at the time.

But he insisted. For what must have been more than an hour, Dennis sat on the linoleum floor with me in that 6-by-6 bathroom, talking, encouraging, and helping as I continued to heave every few minutes.

When I was in school our pastor used to tell us, "The banana that leaves the bunch gets peeled". Now I saw what he meant. I wondered what would have happened if I had isolated myself and taken the attitude that I didn't need anybody. When things were good, I could have done that. But in my hour of need, who would have been there?

I learned so many things from those times. One Sunday afternoon, Dr. Paino called me. I was very sick that day and could not get out of bed. He wanted to let me know that he was thinking of me and that the church would pray for me that night. His call brought great comfort, but I felt guilty because I could not find the strength to pray.

Several weeks later when recovering from treatment I told him of my experience. I was surprised when he didn't reprimand me, but instead he said, "That is why we are here. We are here to pray for others when they can't pray for themselves." What grace and comfort.

In addition, I received cards from all over the nation saying, "We are praying for you" and "Get Well". Many of the cards came from those that I didn't even know.

Tremendous strength was afforded me through the support of others. God uses people who are willing to be used. I want to say thank you to the many who made a difference for me.

"Two {are} better than one; because they have a good reward for their labour." "For if they fall, the one will lift up his fellow: but woe to him {that is} alone when he falleth; for {he hath} not another to help him up." "Again, if two lie together, then they have heat: but how can one be warm {alone}?" "And if one prevail against him, two shall withstand him; and a threefold cord is not quickly broken." Ecclesiastes 4:9-12

Chapter Seven

THE VALLEY OF DISCOURAGEMENT

"Doctor Meyers, I don't think that I can take any more of this. Any more "chemo" and I think that I will die."

As the doctor replied I felt the room begin to spin around me. My knees began to buckle and I felt panicky on the inside. What was happening to me? If this was not dying, then it was the closest thing to it.

He dialogued that indeed I was dying. He told me that death is exactly what they wanted to accomplish. He said that three more courses of "chemo" would kill me. Wow! There was death in me in two ways. Cancer and "Chemo".

I realized that there is a real message in that statement to the body of Christ. I felt so bad that I was tempted to give up. Discouragement had set in. I felt bad, looked bad, couldn't socialize, couldn't pray, read, attend church, or even play with my children. I had lost my right testicle and bills were piling up.

Discouragement is a common problem for all of us. The children of Israel became discouraged when they were rebuilding Jerusalem's walls.

"And Judah said, The strength of the bearers of burdens is decayed, and {there is} much rubbish; so that we are not able to build the wall." "And our adversaries said, they shall not know, neither see, till we come in the midst among them, and slay them, and cause the work to cease." "And it came to pass, that

*when the Jews which dwelt by them came, they said
unto us ten times, from all places whence ye shall
return unto us {they will be upon you}."
Nehemiah 4:10-12*

They were halfway finished, but now were
discouraged. I began to realize that discouragement is a
temporary but deadly condition of the mind. If I continued
to entertain those thoughts and feelings, it would produce a
death grip in me. The greatest enemy in life and faith is
discouragement. I discovered that it was critical that I deal
with it. There were too many unfinished projects in my life
because of it. I couldn't afford not to finish this one.

I want to share with you the path to overcoming
discouragement.

12 Steps to Overcoming Discouragement

1. Don't Quit

*"Therefore be ye also ready: for in such an hour as ye
think not the Son of man cometh." Matthew 24:44
"Watch ye, stand fast in the faith, quit you like men, be
strong." 1 Corinthians 16:13*

2. Dare to Believe

*" If you can believe, all things {are} possible
to him that believeth." Mark 9:23*

3. Deflect Cynical Thoughts

"I beseech you therefore, brethren, by the mercies

of God, that ye present your bodies a living sacrifice, holy, acceptable unto God, {which is} your reasonable service." "And be not conformed to this world: but be ye transformed by the renewing of your mind, that ye may prove what {is} that good, and acceptable, and perfect, will of God." Romans 12:1-2

4. Declare You Will Make It

"And Jesus answering saith unto them, Have faith in God." "For verily I say unto you, That whosoever shall say unto this mountain, Be thou removed, and be thou cast into the sea; and shall not doubt in his heart, but shall believe that those things which he saith shall come to pass; he shall have whatsoever he saith." "Therefore I say unto you, What things soever ye desire, when ye pray, believe that ye receive {them}, and ye shall have {them}." Mark 11:22-24

5. Decide to Go Forward

"And Jesus said unto him, No man, having put his hand to the plough, and looking back, is fit for the kingdom of God." Luke 9:57-62

6. Determine Your Direction

"Where {there is} no vision the people perish: but he that keepeth the law, happy {is} he." Proverbs 29:18 "And the Lord answered me, and said, Write the vision, and make {it} plain upon tables, that he may run that readeth it." Habbukkuk 2:2

7. Deliver Yourself from Your Past

"Be ye angry, and sin not: let not the sun go down upon your wrath: Neither give place to the devil. Let all bitterness, and wrath, and anger, and clamour, and evil speaking, be put away from you, with all malice: And be ye kind one to another, tenderhearted forgiving one another, even as God for Christ's sake hath forgiven you." Ephesians 4:26,27,31,32

8. Develop Friendships with Overcomers

"After these things the Lord appointed other seventy also, and sent them two and two before his face into every city and place, whither he himself would come." Luke 10:1
"Wherefore come out from among them, and be ye separate, saith the Lord, and touch not the unclean {thing}; and I will receive you." 2 Corinthians 6:17

9. Demand Grace from Yourself for Yourself

"If we confess our sins, he is faithful and just to forgive us {our} sins, and to cleanse us from all unrighteousness. 1 John 1:9
"For if our heart condemn us, God is greater than our heart, and knoweth all things." 1 John 3:20

10. Descend Your Pride

"Humble yourselves therefore under the mighty hand of God, that he may exalt you in due time:" 1 Peter 5:6

11. Distinguish Your Source

"Looking unto Jesus the author and finisher of {our} faith; who for the joy that was set before him endured the cross, despising the shame, and is set down at the right hand of the throne of God."   *Hebrews 12:2*

12. Deepen Your Commitment To God

"Trust in the Lord, and do good; {so} shalt thou dwell in the land, and verily thou shalt be fed."   *"Delight thyself also in the Lord: and he shall give thee the desires of thine heart."*   *"Commit thy way unto the Lord; trust also in him; and he shall bring {it} to pass."   Psalm 37:1-11*

I was discouraged, although I was given hope and headed for the finish line. I knew deep down that I could not quit what I had started. One of my fellow ministers and friends, Phil Paino, was in a car accident in 1985 that left him paralyzed from the waist down. When the doctors gave him his prognosis, they said that he would be bound to a wheelchair all of his life.

But Phil was a fighter. He looked until he found someone who would help him walk. It required painful therapy for the first five hours of each day and canes to balance himself. He worked hard until he was able to walk and not ride.

While I was suffering with cancer, Phil wrote me a letter. He was still in therapy five hours a day and walking on canes. But he wanted to encourage me. I was amazed at his courage and selflessness. To this day I am impressed with the fact that he has not allowed hindrances to discourage or defeat him. He continues to walk toward the finish line.

Like a runner in a race, the Bible teaches that we need to continue to the end. If we do, there is a crown of righteousness that will be given to us by the Lord Himself.

If you find yourself discouraged, hindered, tired, or ready to quit, DON'T! Go on. It's worth it.

Chapter Eight

THE VALLEY WITH JOY

"I just don't want to face this again."

My friend, Pat, had just called to ask my advice. She received word that her cancer had recurred. She was distraught. After we talked and prayed, I sat down to write this chapter. I was reminded of the pain and grief. The feelings of fear and frustration returned as I identified with her situation. I began to weep for her. Then as we finished praying, she wept and giggled at the same time. Behind that pain, I heard joy.

In the midst of such heartache and difficulty, how can a person be sustained? Only through the development of joy. Joy was a source of strength! It is not a circumstance or a feeling. It is a characteristic that is developed by walking closely to God.

In his book, "You've Gotta Keep Dancin'", Tim Hansel makes a great statement concerning joy in the midst of pain and sorrow.

"Pain is inevitable, but misery is optional."

In this book I have attempted to share my pain for the benefit of others who suffer. But it is not my desire to share misery. That is optional. The difference is in attitude.

Even in the midst of pain, we can choose to have joy. It comes to us from an awareness of God's presence in our lives.

"In your presence is fullness of JOY" Psalm 16:11
"the fruit of the Spirit is ...JOY...". Galatians 5:22

It always helps when we can laugh. I appreciated that

my friends did not treat me as if I was a holy object that could no longer have a good time. Though limited, I still wanted to see Bill Cosby tell a joke, chuckle, and find humor in the day's circumstances. Laughter relieves the stress level. It brings us healing.

Yet, in my weakness from chemotherapy I didn't even have the strength to laugh. For three months I couldn't, but I had joy.

One night a friend came to visit. To comfort me, he brought a video tape of Bill Cosby telling stories of how babies are born. It was hillarious. I began to laugh uncontrollably. But after a few minutes I had to leave the room. The laughter had zapped my strength and I felt myself exhausted.

But my family spent the night finding healing in the joy of laughter. Sometimes those close to a cancer patient need the healing and release that laughter affords.

There have been many medical studies on the value of humor in the healing process. I know that it helped me always to feel better and to find courage to face the tasks and fears that cancer presented.

"A merry heart doeth good like a medicine."
Proverbs 17:22

Joy is the medicine that afforded strength to Alison and me in the valley. The joy of the Lord is our strength!

There is a difference between happiness and joy. Circumstances produce happiness. So happiness depends on circumstances. Joy comes from the Lord.

"And now come I to thee; and these things I speak in the world, that they might have my joy fulfilled in themselves." John 17:13

"Now the God of hope fill you with all joy and peace in believing, that ye may abound in hope, through the power of the Holy Ghost." Romans 15:13

Circumstances, feelings, and life changes cannot take that away. The world cannot give us joy, and it cannot take it away.

In God's economy we can have "longsuffering with joy".

"Strengthened with all might, according to his glorious power, unto all patience and longsuffering with joyfulness;" Colossians 1:11

This is a mystery without a relationship with God through Jesus Christ, but in Christ it is possible. Our difficulty cannot interrupt or destroy our relationship with God. Instead, God uses difficulty to develop our faith and we can "count it all joy".

"My brethren, count it all joy when ye fall into divers temptations;" James 1:2

Spending time daily with the Lord produces "JOY INEXPRESSIBLE".

"Whom having not seen, ye love; in whom, though now ye see {him} not, yet believing, ye rejoice with joy unspeakable and full of glory:" 1 Peter 1:8

In the midst of your circumstance, the joy of the Lord is your strength. It will bring healing.

Chapter Nine

THE VALLEY WITH HOPE

I sat in front of the television. My last treatment had been received. I was still sick, but the doctors said that I would begin to feel better in 3-4 weeks. That didn't change the fact that I felt out of control of my life and I looked like an alien from outer space. The bills had piled up and our income was down. I couldn't sleep at nights. The night became an enemy. I hoped for the break of day.

When daytime came, I waited for night because there was nothing to do. I should have been happy. I knew in my heart that it would be all right, but I couldn't shake the feelings of failure, frustration, and anger. I was depressed and caught myself wishing for death.

As I watched a television movie, someone suffered a violent death. I heard myself say, "They are lucky. They died." Then I snapped out of it and reminded myself that was not right and that I should not accept those thoughts.

From September to December I fought those thoughts and feelings. I wanted to sell our home because of the financial stress. I didn't know where to turn, except the Lord. But I felt dead on the inside. The drugs, chemotherapy, and interruption to life had taken its affect.

In December of that year, a pastor friend invited me to a revival meeting. I didn't know the man who was to speak and he knew nothing of me. After his sermon, he began to call all of the ministers to the altar for prayer. After he prayed for me, he said that the Lord had shown him my life and he began to describe every thought and feeling that tormented me.

Then he believed the Holy Spirit wanted to say to

me that it was all over. The pockets that had been torn and empty would now be sewn up and God would fill those pockets. It was time for me to build the house of God and not to worry because the Lord was with me.

"Ye have sown much, and bring in little; ye eat, but ye have not enough; ye drink, but ye are not filled with drink; ye clothe you, but there is none warm; and he that earneth wages earneth wages {to put it} into a bag with holes." "Thus saith the Lord of hosts; Consider your ways." "Go up to the mountain, and bring wood, and build the house; and I will take pleasure in it, and I will be glorified, saith the Lord". Haggai 1:6-8

Something broke in me as I knew that God was speaking to me. He was not finished with my life. It still had purpose. Heaven wasn't ready for me!

New vision and new strength filled my spirit. I was reminded of Elijah who became depressed after the greatest victory and miracle of his ministry. God met with him as a still small voice. The Lord just gave Elijah his next assignment and the depression lifted. That is what happened to me. It was gone immediately. A new man went home that night to his wife. I was ready to go forward.

In that time of depression, the Lord taught me several things about the power of hope.

Try to remember three truths.

1. God Provides Strength

Sudden loss, change, and a negative report naturally produce shock. As I floated through that day, I felt ashamed that I couldn't shake that lingering sense of emptiness, loneliness, and numbness. It was later that my doctors began to explain that anyone who receives a "blast", physically or mentally, reacts in the same manner.

In the Bible, King David learned of the loss of his best friend, Jonathan. In addition to that, the King of Israel and the armies of Israel lay dead from the battle with the Philistines.

"Then David took hold on his clothes, and rent them; and likewise all the men that {were} with him:"
2 Samuel 1:11

You can only imagine the grief that must have grabbed the hearts of these men. It caused an instant reaction. They tore their clothes at the news of the loss of friends, status, and perceived protectors.

In the Garden of Gethsemane, Jesus found Himself in a soulful disturbance as He faced the cross. He prayed that the Father would remove that bitter cup from His path, if there would be any other way. In the torment of that moment Jesus, [He who was God in the flesh], reacted physically.

"And he was withdrawn from them about a stone's cast, and kneeled down, and prayed," "Saying, Father, if thou be willing, remove this cup from me: nevertheless not my will, but thine, be done." "And there appeared an angel unto him from heaven, strengthening him." "And being in an agony he prayed more earnestly: and his sweat was as it were great drops of blood falling down to the ground." "And when he rose up from prayer, and was come to his disciples, he found them sleeping for sorrow," "And said unto them, Why sleep ye? rise and pray, lest ye enter into temptation." Luke 22:41-46

Notice that in the midst of the agony of Jesus Christ, that the Father strengthened Him by a messenger. It says,

"And there appeared an angel unto him from heaven, strengthening him." (verse 43)

Our human tendency is to see our situation as being God. God is greater than our stress, pain, or circumstances. God is not limited by human and natural limitations.

Life is filled with difficulty, but God is ready to redeem us in the tragedies of life.   When trouble comes, there is strength available for you, in God.

God does know when we hurt and wants to strengthen us. When we can't go on, He carries us.

2. Grief Lasts for a Season

The Bible goes on to say that grief set in on David and his men.

"And they mourned, and wept, and fasted until even, for Saul, and for Jonathan his son, and for the people of the Lord, and for the house of Israel; because they were fallen by the sword." 2 Samuel 1:12

Grief   exists.   No   circumstance,   knowledge, achievement, position, or status in life can remove the reality of the pain of grief. As a pastor, I have often sat with families in their grief. Everyone expresses it in different ways, but all experience grief when a person perceives that they have lost something or someone that is dear to them .

In her book, "On Death and Dying", Elizabeth Kubler-Ross suggest that there are five stages to grief. All who grieve will pass through these phases. Everyone feels pain in each stage. Here is the process:

DENIAL > ANGER > BARGAINING > DEPRESSION > ACCEPTANCE

Christian psychologist, Dr. Stan DeKovan, identifies six stages of grief in his book, "Grief Relief". They are as follows:

1. **Shock** - "With shock, a kind of numbness envelops you."

2. **Denial** - "Of course, you understand intellectually what has happened through your loss, but on a deeper level, all of your habits and memories are denying the death or the loss that has occurred."

3. **Fantasy vs. Reality**

4. **Grief Release** - "Sooner or later you will come to realize that your loss is real, and the pain of this reality will penetrate to your deepest self. You will cry and weep - from deep within your gut. Your feelings will come pouring out like a fountain of sorrow."

5. **Living With the Memories** - "the pain of grief begins to ease."

6. **Acceptance; Affirmation** - "In this stage, you are now beginning to accept the loss and affirm in your own life that you will go on living."

I would like to suggest another stage that is involved:
HOPE!

As you allow God to minister to you, hope will return. This is the distinction of those who grieve without Christ and those who grieve with Him.

"But I do not want you to be ignorant, brethren, concerning those who have fallen asleep, lest you sorrow as others who have no hope."
1 Thessalonians 4:14

When you find yourself dealing with death, loss, and difficulty, it is important that you allow yourself the process of grief. Own the pain and the feelings of anger, despondency, loss, frustration, and fear. Admit to yourself, to God, and to others that you hurt and that you do not like what is happening to you.

It is vitally important that you know that grief is only for a season. David discovered this truth and wrote beautiful and encouraging words in Psalm 30:4-12.

"Sing unto the Lord, O ye saints of his, and give thanks at the remembrance of his holiness." "For his anger {endureth but} a moment; in his favour {is} life: weeping may endure for a night, but joy {cometh} in the morning." "And in my prosperity I said, I shall never be moved." "Lord, by thy favour thou hast made my mountain to stand strong: thou didst hide thy face, {and} I was troubled." "I cried to thee, O Lord; and unto the Lord I made supplication." "What profit {is there} in my blood, when I go down to the pit? Shall the dust praise thee? shall it declare thy truth?" "Hear, O Lord, and have mercy upon me: Lord, be thou my helper." "Thou hast turned for me

my mourning into dancing: thou hast put off my sackcloth, and girded me with gladness;" "To the end that {my} glory may sing praise to thee, and not be silent. O Lord my God, I will give thanks unto thee for ever."

What hope! There is a light at the end of that dark tunnel. The night season affords a new promise from God. Hold on, because God will see you through.

This was illustrated when I was converted to Christianity. In 1970, John Lloyd wanted to reach every hippie in the Midwest for Christ through a coffeehouse called the Adam's Apple in Fort Wayne, Indiana.

This was a wild scene. The floor was covered with carpet samples laid out in a patchwork design. For tables, we used the big spools that the electric company carry wire on. Food was served during intermissions and the place was filled with hippies smoking, joking, and enjoying programs presented on a tiny platform in the corner of the room. To top it all off, they used black lights in the audience for that "special" effect.

At the end of each set before intermission, they would have one of the hippies tell their story of how they became a Christian. Then an invitation was given for others to commit their lives to Christ, also.

As a result, over 1,500 young people committed their lives to Christ in just one summer. Today many thousands of those people are leading and serving in great churches across America because of the Adam's Apple ministry in the decades of the 70's.

I'm thankful for people like John Lloyd and Dr. Paul E. Paino who would walk by faith and make it possible for my wife and I to know and understand the message of God's grace in Jesus Christ.

It all began for me at age sixteen. Broken in my spirit from a breakup with a girlfriend, I turned to drugs and alcohol for comfort. One night while partying, I was beaten up by a 21-year-old in a youthful dispute. The drugs wore off and all of my pain came crashing in on my mind. I was lonely and empty.

That next weekend, looking for more drugs, I went to the Adam's Apple. Instead a friend asked me to attend a prayer meeting. As I sat on the floor listening to people pray, I was impressed with their sincerity and unselfishness. They prayed for others and not for themselves. They prayed as if God would hear them and do something in response.

A man prayed for a teen with a "filthy" mouth. I looked to see if he meant me, but I didn't know the man. I bowed my head. As I closed my eyes, my mind turned into a television screen and I saw my sinful career as a rebellious teen. For the first time I sensed my guilt. Then from the recesses of my memory, I saw the crucifixion scene from the "Greatest Story Ever Told".

Jesus, with blood streaming down His royal face, a crown of thorns on His head, and gasping for breath cried, "Father, forgive them for they know not what they do." Something inside made me know that the Lord was there and would forgive me. I prayed, "Jesus, I am sorry for all I've done wrong. I want to follow you." With that, all of the guilt lifted and a wonderful peace took its place.

I received spiritual life that night. Out of stress, God moved me into a brighter season. The next day, everything was different. I started to swear with my friends when all of a sudden there was a voice talking to me from inside. "I don't want you to say that." I had never heard it before, but I came to know it as the voice of the Holy Spirit. That voice has led and sustained me in every experience of life.

When in the dark seasons of life, God promises that it

will have an end. Light, joy, and reward will follow, if you trust in Him.

3. Good Things Follow the Stress

For years, Dr. Paul E. Paino has emphasized this truth. He says when testing comes, it means that God is about to do something greater in your life. The test is there to prepare you for the next plateau in God.

You must have a death to have a resurrection. Jesus taught us that a grain of wheat must fall to the ground before you can have a harvest.

> *"And Jesus answered them, saying, The hour is come, that the Son of man should be glorified."* *"Verily, verily, I say unto you, Except a corn of wheat fall into the ground and die, it abideth alone: but if it die, it bringeth forth much fruit."* *"He that loveth his life shall lose it; and he that hateth his life in this world shall keep it unto life eternal."* *"If any man serve me, let him follow me; and where I am, there shall also my servant be: if any man serve me, him will {my} Father honour."* *John 12:23-26*

Jesus had to die on a cross before He could raise from the dead. In the same way, something must die in us before we can know the better, more productive elements in life. Greater things come out of the resurrection than you experience in the natural.

When you are in shock over loss, remember that God has a plan. He is about to bless you, develop you, and use your life in a greater way.

CHAPTER TEN

THE VALLEY WITH THE HEALER

The room had faded into darkness. I could not find the strength to turn the lights on. The family had gone to church and I lay in the easy chair with a blue linen robe wrapped about my frail and emaciated body. My body ached from the constant vomiting. My brain felt like it would explode at any moment. In that loneliness, a sense of abandonment began to set in on my mind.

In the midst of this agony and pain, I had only one person to turn to...Jesus. I don't know where I found the strength, but with a muted voice I began to say, "Lord, I love you. I know that you are here. I need you. I want you." With what little energy I had left, I lifted my trembling hands with my deteriorated arms to the Lord.

Suddenly, I felt a surge of the presence of God. It was amazing. I was sick, alone, weak, mentally diminished, incapacitated, and confounded by my circumstances, but the Healer was there with me.

Somehow I sensed that He identified with my circumstance and my suffering. He had arrived to encourage me. In my spirit, I heard the Lord say to my heart, "I am with you. I am here to touch you and take care of you. Don't worry or fret, because I have all things under control. I have not left you. I will not forsake you. I love you."

In that condition I began to ask the Lord questions about healing. If He is the Healer, then why did I have to have chemotherapy?

Some say that sickness indicates sin or lack of faith. Did I sin? Have I lacked faith? Someone quoted an evangelist who said that all cancer was caused by demons. Did I have a demon?

In that quest with the healer, I discovered many wonderful things.

I. The Lord is our Healer

"And said, If thou wilt diligently hearken to the voice of the Lord thy God, and wilt do that which is right in his sight, and wilt give ear to his commandments, and keep all his statutes, I will put none of these diseases upon thee, which I have brought upon the Egyptians: for I {am} the Lord that healeth thee." Exodus 15:26

The phrase literally means, "The LORD our Physician". God said to Israel that if they would obey His laws, that He would spare them the sickness of other nations. That is because God understands what we need to be healthy. Like any doctor, it is in the character of God to promote health. All healing comes from the Lord. Jesus, on earth, was a healer.

"And Jesus went about all Galilee, teaching in their synagogues, and preaching the gospel of the kingdom, and healing all manner of sickness and all manner of disease among the people." Matthew 4:23

He rose from the dead and continues to heal the sick.

"Be it known unto you all, and to all the people of Israel, that by the name of Jesus Christ of Nazareth, whom ye crucified, whom God raised from the dead, {even} by him doth this man stand here before you whole." Acts 4:10

"Is any sick among you? let him call for the elders of the church; and let them pray over him, anointing him with oil in the name of the Lord:"   "And the prayer of faith shall save the sick, and the Lord shall raise him up; and if he have committed sins, they shall be forgiven him."   "Confess {your} faults one to another, and pray one for another, that ye may be healed. The effectual fervent prayer of a righteous man availeth much."   James 5:16

He is the same today as He was yesterday and will be tomorrow.

"Jesus Christ the same yesterday, and today, and forever."   Hebrews 13:8

II. The Lord Heals Miraculously and Wonderfully

Jesus often healed people through supernatural means. Each time He did this, He used different ways.

He healed a blind man by putting mud on His eyes. A woman with an issue of blood received her miracle when she touched the hem of His garment.   At His word, a lame man took up His bed and walked.

The common thread was faith on the part of those that were healed.   When the Lord said that He wanted to heal them, they believed and obeyed whatever He said.

III. The Lord Heals Through Processes

"And as he entered into a certain village, there met him ten men that were lepers, which stood afar off:"   "And they lifted up {their} voices, and said, Jesus, Master, have mercy on us."   "And when he saw

79

{them}, he said unto them, Go shew yourselves unto the priests. And it came to pass, that, as they went, they were cleansed." Luke 17:14-15

Notice the phrase, "as they went". The priest represented the physicians of their culture. All of this suggests a process to which the lepers submitted.

Whatever the healing agent, God is the author. He created all things. When the medical world establishes a cure for a disease, it is because they have discovered some truth about creation and applied it for the sake of healing. In all of this, the Lord is the Healer because He created the agents of healing.

Healthy habits in body and mind are vehicles of healing for God. Prayers of faith and comfort, bring strength and healing. When we yield to God's will, He often directs us to a process of healing.

IV. Sickness is not Always an Indication of Personal Sin or Lack of Faith

"And as {Jesus} passed by, he saw a man which was blind from {his} birth." "And his disciples asked him, saying, Master, who did sin, this man, or his parents, that he was born blind?" "Jesus answered, Neither hath this man sinned, nor his parents: but that the works of God should be made manifest in him. I must work the works of him that sent me, while it is day: the night cometh, when no man can work." John 9:1-4

Bible scholars have indicated that the punctuation of these verses should be corrected. The New Testament was originally written in Greek. In Greek, it had no punctuation.

That was added later for our help when it was translated into English. Here is how the scholars believe it should read.

"Jesus answered, 'Neither hath this man sinned, nor his parents. But that the works of God should be manifest in him, I must work the works of Him that sent me while it is day. The night cometh when no man can work."

Jesus taught His disciples that neither the man nor His parents were guilty of anything that produced the man's blind condition. Again, we see God's character to heal because Jesus brushed aside the need to blame and said that He needed to get to work and heal the man for God's glory.

As human beings, we are under a law of sin and death. That means we are not in the process of living, but of dying. But the good news is that Jesus came to redeem us and as the Healer, He can touch us with His strength and power.

V. The Greatest Miracle is the Spiritual Healing of a Soul

"When Jesus saw their faith, he said unto the sick of the palsy, Son, thy sins be forgiven thee." "But there were certain of the scribes sitting there, and reasoning in their hearts," "Why doth this {man} thus speak blasphemies? who can forgive sins but God only?" "And immediately when Jesus perceived in his spirit that they so reasoned within themselves, he said unto them, Why reason ye these things in your hearts?" "Whether is it easier to say to the sick of the palsy, {Thy} sins be forgiven thee; or to say, Arise, and take up thy bed, and walk?" "But that ye may know that

the Son of man hath power on earth to forgive sins, (he saith to the sick of the palsy,)" "I say unto thee, Arise, and take up thy bed, and go thy way into thine house." "And immediately he arose, took up the bed, and went forth before them all; insomuch that they were all amazed, and glorified God, saying, We never saw it on this fashion."   Mark 2:5-12

When the Lord saw this paralytic, He forgave the man of all sin. This was more important to Jesus and the man's well-being, both temporal and eternal.

When the scribes questioned His authority, Jesus healed the man of the paralysis to prove that He indeed had authority to heal the soul of sin.

The greatest miracle that any of us can ever experience is to know that God has forgiven us of our sin through Jesus Christ. He is willing, when we ask.

VI. Healing is not a Guarantee of Perfect Health

Jesus healed a man named Lazarus by raising Lazarus from the dead. There could be no more wonderful physical healing than that. Yet Lazarus is in the grave today. As a matter of fact, everyone that Jesus healed in the New Testament is in a grave today. Healing, at best, is a temporary fix. That is why we can experience healing in one area of our body and still be sick in another area.

VII. Resurrection is the Greatest and Only Permanent Healing

Lazarus did die, but He will live again in perfect health.

"Jesus said unto her, I am the resurrection, and the life: he that believeth in me, though he were dead, yetshall he live:"   "And whosoever liveth and believeth in me shall never die. Believest thou this?"
John 11:25-26

Jesus promised to give resurrection life to all who believe. Heaven is a real place. There will be no hospitals, police force, mental institutions, or funeral homes there because there will be no sickness, sin, sorrow, or death. Everyone who puts their faith in Jesus as Saviour will live forever with Him.

Perhaps as you read this you are wondering about your loved one who was ill and has died. Please know that God has not failed you, but has another plan. I survived cancer, but more die from this disease than survive. A lack of physical healing is not an indication of rejection.

So what is healing?   It is an advance touch of resurrection life that puts a patch on our condition. But the greatest healing is to live in Heaven with Jesus through death and resurrection.

CHAPTER ELEVEN

THE VALLEY OF DOUBTS

"I'll send a check as soon as I can." The lady on the other end of the line seemed so cynical. She acted as if I was trying to lie to her and get away with some heinous crime. She worked for a collection agency and wanted payment for some of the tests. We were doing our best to recover from all of the bills that we had incurred through the course of treatment, but it didn't seem to matter to her.

As I sat on the L-shaped couch leaning on the smooth silky mauve pillows, I thought of the dozens of conversations that I had with people like her. I told myself, "She's just doing her job. She doesn't know me and can't respond to me as a person or according to my character." Stroking the budding bristles on my bald head, feeling embarrassed, I thought that they should remember that I was a cancer patient, not a drug dealer!

I had tried to keep my debts current. I didn't intend to be in trouble. It just happened. I wondered why I was treated this way.

Reaching for the stack of bills laying on the oak laminated coffee table, I reviewed the figures and tried to calculate if we would ever get through this trial.

The question, "WHY?" began to write like chalk on my consciousness. Nagging doubts began creeping around my head. I didn't believe that God gave me the sickness, yet, God is Almighty. That means that He can protect me from evil and pain. So why did He permit this to happen? Why does evil exist in this world, if God is so good and loving? I didn't ask for this. I thought that if I was a Christian, my life would be full of good things. How could this be good? How could famine victims be in a blessed condition? How can those who are damaged and disturbed in war zones be made to suffer? The good suffer with the evil and sometimes the good suffer because of the evil of others.

These questions drove me for answers. All people have doubts. Believers will doubt. There is no sin in doubting. What we do with doubt determines its effects.

If I allow doubt to discourage me until I turn bitter and lose faith, then it is destructive. If I permit doubt to be an indicator that triggers me to find the truth, then it establishes faith. So I began to ask God why He would allow suffering. Why didn't He prevent it?

This quest brought answers from God's Word. That is where I find comfort and often God speaks to me from the reading of the Bible.

In our trials we:

I. Learn the Comfort of God

"Who comforteth us in all our tribulation, that we may be able to comfort them which are in any trouble, by the comfort wherewith we ourselves are comforted of God." "For as the sufferings of Christ abound in us, so our consolation also aboundeth by Christ." "And whether we be afflicted, {it is} for your consolation and salvation, which is effectual in the enduring of the same sufferings which we also suffer: or whether we be comforted, {it is} for your consolation and salvation." "And our hope of you {is} stedfast, knowing, that as ye are partakers of the sufferings, so {shall ye be} also of the consolation." 2 Corinthians 1:4-7

The verse tells us that it is in all our tribulations

that we receive God's comfort, if we will turn to Him. That means whether the difficulty is cancer, other sickness, financial distress, misunderstanding, divorce, death of a loved one, or failure, that God intends to use the circumstance to teach us His comfort.

The word comfort means counsel or help. In the Greek it is the word "paraklesis". As a military term it pictures two foot soldiers who would stand back to back on the battlefield. The soldier behind you would be your "paraklete", literally the one who covers your back side. As we turn to the Lord in a wilderness experience, He directs us.

God uses our testing times to give us the ability to help others. We are our "brother's keeper". I have found since the adversity of cancer, I have an ability to empathize with those who suffer that I didn't have before. The answers that God gave to me are the helps that I can offer others today. He sent keepers into my life to assist me in my hour of weakness with the lessons they had learned in their own dark days.

The problems prepare us to help others. The greater the degree of difficulty, the greater the preparation to counsel and help others with the comfort of God we have received. Tribulations are the opportunity to learn the comfort of God.

II. Develop Trust in God

"But we had the sentence of death in ourselves, that we should not trust in ourselves, but in God which raiseth the dead:" "Who delivered us from so great a death, and doth deliver: in whom we trust that he will yet deliver {us}." 2 Corinthians 1:9-10

My tendency is to depend on myself and to manipulate my circumstances for my own purposes. But the key to obtaining God's best for my life is surrender.

Affliction puts me in the position that makes me trust God. I found through my cancer experience that I had nothing but God. But when all I had was God, I found that God was enough. God delivered me. In my present I know He does deliver me, because He did deliver me. In my future He will deliver me because God never changes. Problems develop our trust in God.

III. Bring Thanks to God

"Ye also helping together by prayer for us, that for the gift {bestowed} upon us by the means of many persons thanks may be given by many on our behalf."
2 Corinthians 1:10-11

When difficulty came, many others rushed to aid me. Each time they came, I found myself thanking God for their loving service and His grace to supply. They began to thank God for His deliverance in my situation.

David gave thanks for the men who risked their lives to bring him a drink of water.

"And David longed, and said, Oh that one would give me drink of the water of the well of Bethlehem, that {is} at the gate!" "And the three brake through the host of the Philistines, and drew water out of the well of Bethlehem, that {was} by the gate, and took {it}, and {brought} it to David: but David would not {drink} of it, but poured it out to the Lord." "And said, My God forbid it me, that I should do this

thing: shall I drink the blood of these men that have put their lives in jeopardy?   for with {the jeopardy of} their lives they brought it. Therefore he would not drink it.   These things did these three mightiest."   1 Chronicles 11:17-19

Not just any water, but the water of Bethlehem, his home town, that was from the well by the gate. When he saw their love and loyalty, he poured the water on the ground as a praise offering. He couldn't receive this glory and flattery for himself, but felt humbled and grateful for their sacrifice. So David did the only thing that he could. He gave the thanks and praise to God who alone deserved this level of consecration.   Their response created an atmosphere of worship and praise.

The Apostle Paul described the same expeience in his life.

"Yea, and if I be offered upon the sacrifice and service of your faith, I joy, and rejoice with you all." Phillipians 2:17

The New King James Version says,

"Yes, and if I am being poured out as a drink offering on the sacrifice and service of your faith, I am glad and rejoice with you all."

When the Apostle saw the service, sacrfice, and faith of the Phillipian church, he felt obligated to give God thanks, praise, and rejoicing. The church responded to Paul in his time of trial with prayers of deliverance and offerings to support him. Paul's difficulty was an opportunity for praise, thanksgiving, and worship to come to God as God's people dedicated themselves to go forward and believe.

In the midst of difficulties, the Lord will work in people to touch you. When He does, rejoice in the Lord for His work in people. Your circumstance can bring glory to God.

Writing this book has caused me to remember the many volunteers, staff workers, researchers, and medical personel associatied with the American Cancer Society and Indiana University Medical Center in Indianapolis, Indiana. Before 1976, testicular cancer had a 90% mortality rate with less than two years to live. At the writing of this book, my survival has been for seven years. A private health insurance company wrote a health policy for me this year.

In the same way that God gave me the gift of eternal life at His own expense, the death of His Son, so also I have received a cure and extension on my life at the expense of the American Cancer Society and the work of the Medical Center. I never contributed, researched, raised funds, made any effort to cure cancer. At the expense of their time, money, lives, and work, the gift of healing and added years have been given to me. So I am thankful to God for these marvelous servants of healing and medicine.

Thank you, Lord, for the many whom I have never met that provided the refreshing and healing.

Let me encourage you, in your days of difficulty, to bring thanks to God for those that He has provided to be your ministers.

IV. Receive Discipline

"For out of much affliction and anguish of heart I wrote unto you with many tears; not that ye should be grieved, but that ye might know the love which I have more abundantly unto you." 2 Corinthians 2:4

No matter what the trial or its cause, there is a quality of excellence produced in our character if we commit ourselved to the grace of God. Whom the Lord loves, He chastens.

"And ye have forgotten the exhortation which speaketh unto you as unto children, My son, despise not thou the chastening of the Lord, nor faint when thou art rebuked of him:" "For whom the Lord loveth he chasteneth, and scourgeth every son whom he receiveth." "If ye endure chastening, God dealeth with you as with sons; for what son is he whom the father chasteneth not?" "But if ye be without chastisement, whereof all are partakers, then are ye bastards, and not sons." "Furthermore we have had fathers of our flesh which corrected {us}, and we gave {them} reverence: shall we not much rather be in subjection unto the Father of spirits, and live?" "For they verily for a few days chastened {us} after their own pleasure; but he for {our} profit, that {we} might be partakers of his holiness."   Hebrews 12:6

This is not negative, but an indicator of His grace at work in our lives. The ability to receive instruction and correction is the beginning of wisdom. Through this process, God makes us more like Jesus.

V. Learn our Victory is in Christ

"Now thanks {be} unto God, which always causeth us to triumph in Christ"   2 Corinthians 2:14a

God always leads us to victory in Christ. In every

struggle and through all of the hindrances, God gives us the victory. The key to victory is to follow Him through to victory.

When the children of Israel went into the promised land, God promised that He would give them victory over every enemy. But the key to victory was to stay in a position of following the Lord.

"Yet there shall be a space between you and it, about two thousand cubits by measure: come not near unto it, that ye may know the way by which ye must go: for ye have not passed {this} way heretofore." Joshua 3:4

It is easy to run ahead of God, only to find out that we don't know the way. God's presence is the key to our victory. Keep your eyes on the Lord, He will direct you into every victory.

VI. Make Christ Known to Others

"and maketh manifest the savour of his knowledge by us in every place." "For we are unto God a sweet savour of Christ, in them that are saved, and in them that perish:" "To the one {we are} the savour of death unto death; and to the other the savour of life unto life. And who {is} sufficient for these things?" "For we are not as many, which corrupt the word of God: but as of sincerity, but as of God, in the sight of God speak we in Christ." 2 Corinthians 2:14b-17

Fragrances indicate the character of the person. When I was a kid, sometimes I would walk in the house and smell that delicious aroma that meant "fried chicken"! It spoke of the evening and the meal. Sometimes the odor would be overwhelming and make my nose crinkle. Then I knew that sauerkraut was in the pot. As people observe our trials and see the victories that God brings, they become acquainted with God's character in us. It is an opportunity for Christ to be revealed in our lives.

"But when it pleased God, who separated me from my mother's womb, and called {me} by his grace," "To reveal his Son in me, that I might preach him among the heathen;" Galatians 1:15-16

So adversity is an indicator of the power of Jesus Christ. God uses our situation to illustrate His life and power to others. (2 Corinthians 4:7-13)

VII. Develop the Character of Christ

"For our light affliction, which is but for a moment, worketh for us a far more exceeding {and} eternal weight of glory;" "While we look not at the things which are seen, but at the things which are not seen: for the things which are seen {are} temporal; but the things which are not seen {are} eternal." 2 Corinthians 4:17-18

As we respond to pitfalls by turning to God for His answers, we receive a new measure of the glory of God. Each decision to yield to God in our dilemmas affords us an eternal weight of glory. This life is temporary, but our eternal position in God's economy is being determined by today's decisions. As we remain faithful to Him, He keeps the accounts and will reward us accordingly.

"For we must all appear before the judgment seat of Christ; that every one may receive the things {done} in {his} body, according to that he hath done, whether {it be} good or bad." 2 Corinthians 5:10
"Blessed {is} the man that endureth temptation: for when he is tried, he shall receive the crown of life, which the Lord hath promised to them that love him. James 1:12

God in His ability to know all things, allows certain adversities to accomplish a greater purpose in us. When Jesus suffered on the cross, He committed Himself to the one who could save Him.

"Who, when he was reviled, reviled not again; when he suffered, he threatened not; but committed {himself} to him that judgeth righteously" ...
"Wherefore let them that suffer according to the will of God commit the keeping of their souls {to him} in well doing, as unto a faithful Creator." 1 Peter 2:23; 4:19

There is a time to trust the Father. He created us, and does deliver us.

God, in His sovereignty does allow suffering, but only permits in His children that suffering that can be used for the good. We may not understand why God has let our predicament prevail, but we can know that He has everything under control.

CHAPTER TWELVE

THE STRENGTH OF VALLEYS

Many people pray that they will not have to walk through valleys. It is their desire that God would direct them in such a path that they would never experience the descending journey to the depths of sorrow. Many Christians pray that God will keep them on the mountaintop, just as Peter did in Matthew 17.

Yet, it is in the valley that we receive what we cannot receive any other place.

Cancer caused me to grow as a person. All valleys of life will produce qualities not found in high experiences.

1. In the valley we find food to grow on.

Valleys are filled with fertile areas where foods can grow to bring nourishment and strength to us. You can't find it on the mountaintop, but only in the valley.

No one can grow into the person that God created them to be without proper nourishment and food. God has a way of taking us into the valley so that He can bring to us the strength and nourishment that we won't find on the mountaintop.

2. In the valley we find water.

Valleys are filled with streams and rivers that carry the life and vitality that we all need for an interesting life.

Even in a desert place, if you are willing to work, you can dig wells that will produce the streams of fresh, pure water that your life craves and needs.

Abraham, Isaac, and Jacob all dug wells. These wells became landmarks of their relationship to the Lord and His will. Because they dug a well, they found water.

"Blessed is the man whose strength is in You, whose heart is set on pilgrimage. As they pass through the Valley of Baca, they make it a spring; the rain also covers it with pools." Psalm 84:5-6

Wow, these guys dug wells that both produced springs and turned storms into supply!

"They go from strength to strength; each one appears before God in Zion." Psalm 84:7

The valley brings water that grants strength after strength. Even more, it brings us into the presence of God. Such deep communion can only be known in the valley. This communion produces hope in our lives. The valley does become a place of hope and victory.

"Sharon shall be a fold of flocks, and the Valley of Achor a place for herds to lie down, for My people who have sought Me." Isaiah 65:10

The word "Achor" means "Hope". There is a place of difficulty that God appoints to produce hope. Everytime we pass through or are reminded of it, it will bring hope to our hearts. This passage indicates that in this place, we will have safety, security, and provision.

"I will give her her vineyards from there, and the Valley of Achor as a door of hope; she shall sing there, as in the days of her youth, as in the day when she

came up from the land of Egypt." Hosea 2:15

The valley can be the very passageway that will move you into fulfillment of your desires and all that God has promised you.

The valley can afford water that cleanses, refreshes, restores, and invigorates. It is the valley that gives us the very essence of life itself.

God appoints us to the valley to bring us to the still waters where we can drink and receive what we couldn't receive on the mountaintop.

3. In the valley we receive relationships.

Have you ever noticed that mountaintops are sparsely populated? Why? It is hard to find the necessities of life there. Oh, the scenery is great, the air is fresh, but friendships are few and small in variety.

Valleys are full of people and potential. Though we all resist the valley and feel alone in it, there is more company in the valley than on the mountaintop. In the valley we receive relationships. People that bless you. People that surprise you with their talents, wisdom, gifts, and generosity.

God has other relationships for you. He wants to expand your relationships. In the valley you find friends that you would not know any other way except that you have walked with them in the valley. These people have a way of shaping our lives and character.

"As iron sharpens iron, so a man sharpens the countenance of his friend." Proverbs 27:17

These friends will be your true riches in life.

"A friend loves at all times, and a brother is born for adversity." Proverbs 17:17

True friends are found in the valley and will be there in every circumstance.

Brothers represent what is comfortable and familiar. You like it because it is there, but in time it is due to produce adversity. God wants to give you other relationships.

The greatest friend is to be found in the valley. Solomon goes on to say,

"A man who has friends must himself be friendly, but there is a friend who sticks closer than a brother." Proverbs 18:24

That friend is Jesus Christ. He wants to have a friendship with everyone who will recognize His presence. He is the most important friend of your life. The valley makes us aware of His presence and love.

4. In the valley we receive revelation.

There are many things that grow and live in the valley that cannot grow and live on the mountaintop. I enjoy traveling in a car.

I like it because it gives me an opportunity to see places, people, landscape, buildings, animal life, vegetation, and waterways that I've never seen before. It is an adventuresome time of discovery filled with the blessing of expanding my horizon.

Growing up in northern Indiana, I never saw mountains. We didn't travel for vacations because a family of seven on a school teacher's salary had to be always aware of finances.

That first trip that I made was exhilarating. Alison and I were newlyweds. Christian Training Center, our fellowship's Bible College, was sponsoring a short term mission trip to Mexico. It was a thrill!

Every little thing caught my attention. Highways looked different as we drove through the Ozark Mountains towards Tulsa. I never knew that roads were cut through hills and mountains. The sides were a jagged wall decorated with limestone. The highway unraveled like ribbon into huge valleys ahead.

Colors of gold covered the fields of wheat that met the blue horizons of Oklahoma as we continued. Texas was the biggest, driest, most wind-blown expanse that I had ever experienced.

As we entered Mexico at Juarez, the whole world changed. Some call it culture shock. I'll never forget the smell of open sewage that slapped my nostrils for the first time. I can't forget the woman, aged, missing half of her front teeth, begging for money with a pathetic glance that oozed out the slits called eyes packaged in leathery, wrinkled skin. Never can I put out of my mind the man who cursed us because we didn't give him our goods. This didn't happen in Fort Wayne, Indiana!

In the same way adversity shows us what we couldn't see. Peter on the Mt. of Transfiguration saw such glory in the presence of Elijah, Moses, and the Lord. In the mind of a Jewish man from the shores of Galilee, it couldn't get any better than this. He was caught up in the atmosphere when he said, "Let's build tents. One for Moses, Elijah, and for Jesus." He got so carried away with his own idea that the Lord had to perform an incredible miracle to slow him down.

Why? Because Peter and the disciples needed a

greater revelation of the Lord than the one they received on the mountaintop. There they caught a glimpse of the overall vision, the plan, the dream of God. On the mountain they saw that Jesus was the fulfillment of the law and prophets. Indeed they saw the power of the Kingdom come to earth.

However, they needed to know the character and way of the Kingdom. So God interrupted this fabulous fantasy and made them head down the mountain to the valley once again.

When they arrived in the valley, they were faced with their own powerlessness. Look at the story in Matthew 17:15-17.

"Lord, have mercy on my son, for he is an epileptic and suffers severely: for he often falls into the fire and often into the water. So I brought him to Your disciples, but they could not cure him."

The vision of power of the mountaintop could not produce in them the understanding of the power of the Kingdom. That came in the valley.

"Because of your unbelief: for assuredly, I say to you, if you have faith as a mustard seed, you will say to this mountain, 'move from here to there, and it will move; and nothing will be impossible for you."
Matthew 17:20

The Lord brought deliverance. More importantly He taught the disciples the need for fasting and prayer to experience the power of the Kingdom.

That is just one example of the many things learned in the valley. As the disciples followed the Lord in the valley, it became a backdrop to illustrate truth, communion, crucifixion, resurrection, the church, and the second coming of Christ. The valley is always filled with revelation.

5. In the valley we receive victory.

The mountaintop looms as a place where great fortresses of protection abound. You can experience tremendous comfort and peace there because the surroundings are familiar and comfortable.

However, the fortress lays vulnerable to the enemy through siege. The foe surrounds the fortress, then cuts off food, water, and other supplies. Oh, you still have the fortress, the comfort zone, the familiar, but the vital substances for life dissipate moment by moment. Soon you wake up to realize that the important stock is depleted and unavailable.

Married couples experience this. When first dating, the man makes all the extra efforts. He writes love notes. He calls his gal silly but affectionate names. He buys her flowers. He takes a bath, shaves, and smells good before seeing her. The man always compliments and encourages her.

After marriage, he reaches the comfort zone. He says, "Ah, she's mine. I have her." Now starts the crisis because the tendency is to take her for granted. No more love notes. No more silly but affectionate names. No more flowers. He doesn't keep himself clean, shaves only when he has to and smells like a sewer rat most of the time. Instead of conversation, there is a remote control and newspaper. The enemy defeats you without firing a shot.

The result is a lonely wife who feels insecure, neglected and angry. Now the communication diminishes and the relationship becomes a frustration instead of a blissful and fulfilling union. Trouble is present. The man doesn't know why. His bride can't see why he isn't more sensitive.

Now the siege of the enemy begins. But the difficulty becomes the signal from God that we need to make an effort to remain secure. There is a battle to fight in order to have victory.

In order to face and be delivered from an enemy, you must go into the valley. The enemy lurks in those lowlands and must be rooted out before he has an opportunity to lay siege on you and those that you love. So God, by His grace, leads us to appointed battles with those destroyers of our souls to give us victory.

Some people are deceived to think that you can win through compromise. They only allow you to think that you will be vulnerable to their attack.

The enemies of our lives do not cooperate. Someone has said wisely, "There is no peace without victory." In order to obtain the victory there must be a battle where the adversary is confronted, defeated, and turned away.

James said,

"Resist the devil and he will flee from you."
James 4:7b

To build walls of separation around myself that close off my life from relationships is not victory, rather it is annihilation. The temptation to isolate myself presents seeming comfort because all conflicts come from relationships in my world. However, to run from the conflict guarantees failure and robs me of the riches that God intended for me.

Once I allow the opponent to lay siege, I have given that antagonist control of my life. The tools of the archenemy are fear, unbelief, and ignorance. The Lord wants to free us from any and all restrictions of the tormentor. (I John 4:18; 2 Corinthians 4:4; John 8:31-32)

Jesus intends to grant success to all who will follow Him. He often appoints the valley for the battle, so that we can know conquest. His will is freedom, not control by any circumstance, feeling, or fear. We are to continue in His Word and to follow Him. So what appears negative in the natural, becomes God's occasion to teach us, strengthen us, and to empower us to do His will.

A FIFTEEN MINUTE GUIDE FOR THOSE WHO SUFFER

When you find yourself in a season of pain, grief, and dilemma, I suggest that you remember:

1. GOD PROVIDES STRENGTH

"And he said unto me, My grace is sufficient for thee: for my strength is made perfect in weakness. Most gladly therefore will I rather glory in my infirmities, that the power of Christ may rest upon me.
2 Corinthians 12:9

2. IT'S OKAY TO GRIEVE...FOR JUST A SEASON

"For his anger {endureth but} a moment; in his favour {is} life: weeping may endure for a night, but joy {cometh} in the morning. Psalm 30:5

3. CLING TO GOD'S HOPE

"For I know the thoughts that I think toward you, saith the Lord, thoughts of peace, and not of evil, to give you an expected end." Jeremiah 29:11

4. DEAL WITH YOUR PROBLEMS AND SITUATIONS ASAP

"A wise {man} feareth, and departeth from evil: but the fool rageth, and is confident." Proverbs 14:6

5. UNDERSTAND THAT HELP IS AVAILABLE

"Blessed {be} God, even the Father of our Lord Jesus Christ, the Father of mercies, and the God of all comfort;" "Who comforteth us in all our tribulation, that we may be able to comfort them which are in any trouble, by the comfort wherewith we ourselves are comforted of God." 2 Corinthians 1:3-4

6. DO NOT DENY YOUR SITUATIONS

"Confess {your} faults one to another, and pray one for another, that ye may be healed. The effectual fervent prayer of a righteous man availeth much." James 5:16

7. YOU CAN OVERCOME FEAR

"There is no fear in love; but perfect love casteth out fear: because fear hath torment. He that feareth is not made perfect in love." 1 John 4:18
Forasmuch then as the children are partakers of flesh and blood, he also himself likewise took part of the same; that through death he might destroy him that had the power of death, that is, the devil;" "And

deliver them who through fear of death were all their lifetime subject to bondage." Hebrews 2:14-15

8. PRAYER IS THE FOUNDATION OF YOUR HEALING

"Ask, and it shall be given you; seek, and ye shall find; knock, and it shall be opened unto you:" Matthew 7:7
"And this is the confidence that we have in him, that, if we ask any thing according to his will, he heareth us:" "And if we know that he hear us, whatsoever we ask, we know that we have the petitions that we desired of him." 1 John 5:14-15

9. LET FAITH ARISE WITHIN YOU

"For verily I say unto you, That whosoever shall say unto this mountain, Be thou removed, and be thou cast into the sea; and shall not doubt in his heart, but shall believe that those things which he saith shall come to pass; he shall have whatsoever he saith." "Therefore I say unto you, What things soever ye desire, when ye pray, believe that ye receive {them}, and ye shall have {them}." Mark 11:23-24

10. INTIMATELY RELATE TO GENUINE FRIENDS

"Where no counsel {is}, the people fall: but in the multitude of counselors {there is} safety." Proverbs 11:14

11. DO NOT MAKE HASTY DECISIONS...
    LET GOD SPEAK TO YOU

"Without counsel, plans go awry, but in the multitude of counselors they are established." Proverbs 15:22

12. THOUGHTS DETERMINE YOUR
    ATTITUDE, EMOTION, AND DIRECTION

"For the weapons of our warfare {are} not carnal, but mighty through God to the pulling down of strong holds;" "Casting down imaginations, and every high thing that exalteth itself against the knowledge of God, and bringing into captivity every thought to the obedience of Christ;" 2 Corinthians 10:4-5

13. GOD ALWAYS HAS A BETTER PLAN,
    GOD SEES THE BIG PICTURE. HE HAS
    THE FINAL WORD.

*"My help {cometh} from the Lord, which made heaven and earth." "He will not suffer thy foot to be moved: he that keepeth thee will not slumber."
Psalm 121:2-3*

14. YOUR WORDS RELEASE THE LORD'S
    MINISTRY IN YOUR LIFE

*"Death and life {are} in the power of the tongue: and they that love it shall eat the fruit thereof."
Proverbs 18:21*

"Wherefore, holy brethren, partakers of the heavenly calling, consider the Apostle and High Priest of our profession, Christ Jesus;"   Hebrews 3:1

15. GET ON WITH YOUR LIFE!

"Brethren, I count not myself to have apprehended: but {this} one thing {I do}, forgetting those things which are behind, and reaching forth unto those things which are before."   "I press toward the mark for the prize of the high calling of God in Christ Jesus."
Philippians 3:13-14

16. ALL HEALING COMES FROM GOD

"And said, If thou wilt diligently hearken to the voice of the Lord thy God, and wilt do that which is right in his sight, and wilt give ear to his commandments, and keep all his statutes, I will put none of these diseases upon thee, which I have brought upon the Egyptians: for I {am} the Lord that healeth thee. Exodus 15:26 "Who forgiveth all thine iniquities; who healeth all thy diseases;"   Psalm 103:3

17. GOD ... AND YOU ... ARE VICTORIOUS!

"Nay, in all these things we are more than conquerors through him that loved us."   "For I am persuaded, that neither death, nor life, nor angels, nor principalities, nor powers, nor things present, nor things to come," "Nor height, nor depth, nor any other creature, shall be able to separate us from the love of God, which is in Christ Jesus our Lord."   Romans 8:37-39

Special Thanks To:

Dr. Paul E. Paino, our Bishop and friend, for encouragement and insight.

Mrs. Mary Paino, our spiritual mother, for proofreading.

Dr. Stan DeKovan, Vision University, for input and inspiration.

Dr. Patrick Loehr, Indiana University, for medical help, proofing the medical facts, and support.

Lynn Steller, my secretary, for her tireless hours of typing transcripts.

Stephanie Pyles, our friend, for typesetting and proofing.

Rev. Bob Armstrong, our friend and editor, for his hard work, joyful spirit, and careful undertaking of this project.

- NOTES -

- NOTES -

- NOTES -

- NOTES -

- NOTES -

- NOTES -

- NOTES -

- NOTES -

If this book has been a blessing to you, or if we can be of service to you, please contact us at:

Light For Life Ministries
P. O. Box 755
Auburn, IN 46706